cross
WORDS
A Devotional for Youth

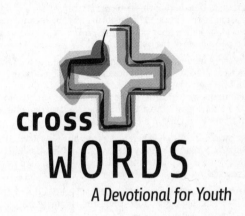

cross
WORDS
A Devotional for Youth

DUANA CISNEY

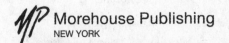
Morehouse Publishing
NEW YORK

Unless otherwise noted, Scripture taken from the Common English Bible®, CEB® Copyright © 2010, 2011 by Common English Bible.™ Used by permission. All rights reserved worldwide. The "CEB" and "Common English Bible" trademarks are registered in the United States Patent and Trademark Office by Common English Bible. Use of either trademark requires the permission of Common English Bible.

Scripture quotations contained herein are from the New Revised Standard Version Bible, copyright © 1989 by the Division of Christian Education of the National Council of Churches of Christ in the U.S.A. Used by permission. All rights reserved.

Scripture marked The Message are from *THE MESSAGE*. Copyright © by Eugene H. Peterson 1993, 1994, 1995, 1996, 2000, 2001, 2002. Used by permission of Tyndale House Publishers, Inc.

Scripture quotations marked (NIV) are taken from the Holy Bible, New International Version®, NIV®. Copyright © 1973, 1978, 1984, 2011 by Biblica, Inc.™ Used by permission of Zondervan. All rights reserved worldwide. www.zondervan.com The "NIV" and "New International Version" are trademarks registered in the United States Patent and Trademark Office by Biblica, Inc.™

Morehouse Publishing, 19 East 34th Street, New York, NY 10016

Morehouse Publishing is an imprint of Church Publishing Incorporated. www.churchpublishing.org

Cover design by Laurie Klein Westhafer, Bounce Design
Typeset by Beth Oberholtzer Design

Library of Congress Cataloging-in-Publication Data

Names: Cisney, Duana, author.
Title: Crosswords : a devotional for youth / Duana Cisney.
Description: New York : Morehouse Pub., 2016.
Identifiers: LCCN 2015044070 (print) | LCCN 2015050014 (ebook) | ISBN 9780819232458 (pbk.) | ISBN 9780819232465 ()
Subjects: LCSH: Christian teenagers—Prayers and devotions. | Christian youth—Prayers and devotions.
Classification: LCC BV4850 .C54 2016 (print) | LCC BV4850 (ebook) | DDC 242/.63—dc23
LC record available at http://lccn.loc.gov/2015044070

Printed in the United States of America

To my husband, Rich,
who patiently read and reread every page
and encouraged this work,
knowing I could do it long before I did.

Contents

Contents

Acknowledgments

I wish to personally thank the following people; each of you has been a positive influence in different and unique ways. I am so very blessed to have you in my life and I thank you for your part in this work being possible.

My husband, Rich: for putting his journalism skills and his heart into this work with me.

My children, Michael, Samantha, and Alexandra: for working through sample devotions and being quiet during those long hours of writing when we could have been doing something more fun.

My mom, Peggy: who has forever been my cheerleader and encouraged me when I was in doubt.

My aunt, Susie (aka "Poof"): from whom I have learned the art of storytelling.

Our godmother, Mommy Gayle: who has been my prayer support in life.

My editor, Sharon Ely Pearson: who took a chance on an idea.

Foreword

Praying shapes believing. This truism, a translation of Prosper of Aquitaine's *Lex orandi, lex credendi*, states succinctly what we all know: It is through prayer practiced over time that we come to know God, who created the world and invites us to a life of discipleship. I recently met a young teenager who grounds her life in daily prayer. She explained that when she comes home from school each day she says the Lord's Prayer and reflects on the day. And she prays more on busy days. There were more things to reflect about! She spoke with confidence that God knows, loves, and calls her to good things. Her trust in God spilled into all of her life. Cultivated by prayer, she embodies her faith. As this teenager shows us, we do not think ourselves into faith.

This beautiful book by Duana Cisney provides teens a way to pray and reflect deeply on their everyday life throughout the year. *Cross Words* is a teen's prayer companion—both in the text and Duana. Prayer is not a lofty, but gritty endeavor. Duana knows teens and doesn't shy away from the real stuff of life. For example, a portion of Week 44's reflection:

Have you ever met anyone that has to be right all the time, correcting everything you say? Have you ever been that way?

Who hasn't? But who's willing to say so before God? God desires *all* of our being, even those things that we aren't so proud of. After each reflection, Duana shows God's faithfulness and love with prayers of encouragement, consolation, and affirmation to hold onto through the week. On Week 44, she prays for easy conversations. This prayer can then be in their back pockets to face difficult conversations. Prayer demands an investment of self—the offering of life itself. And Duana provides ample space for journaling and helpful prompts that relate to the theme of the week to get started.

The lives of teens are governed by many things—marked with stresses and joys, while also drawn into a culture of consumerism. This book offers an alternative rhythm of life—the life of Christ as experienced in the liturgical year. Time, punctuated by the life of Christ, plunges the everyday into waters of the sacred, sustaining the cycles of friendship, academics, sports, and family with God's renewing love. We often forget that in Advent we learn to wait, Epiphany to notice, Lent to take stock, and Easter to celebrate. With this rhythm of the year, teens can enter into the epic narrative of the life in Christ. Weaving daily into this sacred cycle, Duana helps teens see that their own lives are times of sacred waiting, watching, reflection, and celebration.

Praying shapes believing. Over fifty-two weeks, teens have a prayer partner in Duana. Through this book, she will be a companion for teens to ground their lives knowing God's enduring love throughout the year. God is patient, waiting to hear, and eager to see what is yet to be revealed on these pages of prayer.

Jenifer Gamber
All Saints' Day

Introduction

I believe it's important for Scripture to be approachable to students dealing with real life. No matter how far and wide I searched, I couldn't find anything that made the connection between "my best friend is talking bad about me" and Jesus, so I set about trying to fill the gap. This book is a result of my searching, a labor of love born from weekly "e-newsletters" to the youth and their families of churches where I have served.

News of him spread even more and huge crowds gathered to listen and to be healed from their illnesses. But Jesus would withdraw to deserted places for prayer.

Luke 5:15–16

Even in the midst of busyness, Jesus would make time for prayer alone. Jesus gave us an example of how we could create a practice of spiritual nourishment through prayer. *Cross Words* has been created in such a way that each week's devotion can be digested daily, over a few days, or a week. I invite you to read the weekly devotion and then write your initial thoughts. Take some time to sit with what you have read and written. Come back the next day, reread the entry and your words, and then respond to the prompts that I call "Touchstones" that follow.

How This Book Is Organized

- The year is organized by month, starting in January, but you can pick this up at any time to begin to pray and jour-nal. The months are listed in the context of where they fit on the church's calendar year. Some weeks will focus on the church season; some will focus on an event that often occurs around that time of year, such as Valentine's Day or Thanksgiving. There are extra days added for Holy Week, since this is a particular time of the year that Chris-tians set aside time for prayer.

- At the beginning of each month you will see a calendar wheel of all the church's liturgical (worship) seasons. A prayer will be offered from the Book of Common Prayer to start the month and its theme.

- At the beginning of each week, the calendar wheel will be shaded so that you know where we are in the church's cycle, which in some ways is very different than our day-to-day calendar that we may use for school or work.

- Each week begins with a reflection followed by a short piece of Scripture, called "Consider This." A prayer for you for the coming week follows.

- There are several pages that follow, called "Touchstones," that give you an opportunity to journal and reflect. "Initial Thoughts" will get you started, and then throughout the week (or all in one sitting), you can practice "Going Deeper," with additional simple prompts and space for you to continue to write. Lastly, there is "My Reflections," a section for you to add your own thoughts as to how the devotion has called you to view things differently or supported you during the week.

How to Use This Book

- Use the weekly reading to prepare for your coming week.

- Use the prayer given to you and allow it to remain with you all week long. Add your prayers to it as you feel called. Taking time to jot down a word or phrase can help keep important thoughts in mind as you go through your week.

- Use the questions in "Touchstones" throughout the week, responding to one question each day.

Above all, this is an open invitation for you to create a rhythm of prayer that works for you. My prayer is that *Cross Words* will help you know God's love for you in all that you do.

Duana Cisney
The Feast of St. Francis

January

O God our heavenly Father, you have blessed us and given us dominion over all the earth: Increase our reverence before the mystery of life; and give us new insight into your purposes for the human race, and new wisdom and determination in making provision for its future in accordance with your will; through Jesus Christ our Lord. Amen.

Collect for the Future of the Human Race, BCP, 828

In our liturgical calendar:

- January 1—The Holy Name of Our Lord Jesus Christ
- January 6—The Feast of the Epiphany
- The Season of Epiphany

In our secular calendar:

- January 1—New Year's Day
- 3rd Monday in January—Martin Luther King Day

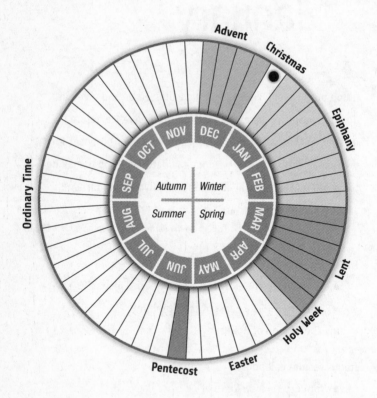

Week 1: A New Year

For many people, the New Year always brings thoughts of the tradition of having a "New Year's Resolution." I like the New Year and the fresh start it brings, but I don't really like the New Year's resolution part. It feels like we're setting ourselves up for failure because, the truth is, most people don't keep their resolutions past the first couple of months of the year.

Consider This:

Even though we once knew Christ from a human point of view, we know him no longer in that way. So if anyone is in Christ, there is a new creation: everything old has passed away; see, everything has become new!

2 Cor. 5:16b–17 NRSV

What if we took the time at the beginning of a new year to reflect on ourselves as the beloved children of God that we are? What if we really looked at ourselves as God does: through the lens of pure love, unconditional and freely given? We would see a new creation—every time! There is nothing that can remove us from the love God has for us except for us. We can never go so far down the wrong road that we can't turn around and find God right there.

Praying you see Christ creating something new in you this week . . .

≡ Touchstones

Initial thoughts:

▓ Going Deeper

Things that keep me from seeing myself as God's beloved:

Things that make me feel unworthy:

How would God respond to me feeling unworthy?

Ways I can accept that I am God's beloved:

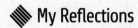 **My Reflections**

JANUARY

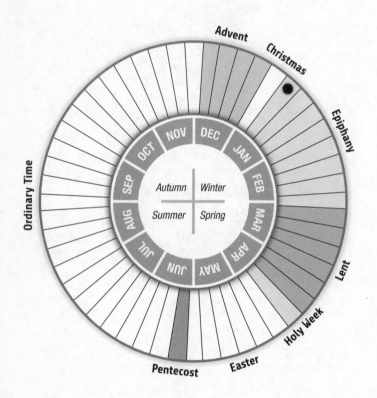

Week 2: Epiphany 1

Have you ever been asked to do something that you felt completely unqualified to do?

I heard Bethany Hegedus, the author of *Grandfather Gandi*[1] talk about her experience in writing the book that began over ten years ago. It's about Ghandi's grandson, Arun (the person with whom she collaborated to write the story). She said that when she started this process, she didn't really have the writing credentials; that she felt unqualified. When she shared those feeling with Arun and asked why he wanted to work with her on it, he said, "Just that you have the heart for this work makes you qualified."

Consider This:

The council was caught by surprise by the confidence with which Peter and John spoke. After all, they understood that these apostles were uneducated and inexperienced. They also recognized that they had been followers of Jesus.

Acts 4:13

There is an old saying, "God doesn't call the qualified, God qualifies the called." On the surface that statement might sound trite, but I think it's deeper than that. I think it means that we don't need to be a certain age, have particular degrees, certifications, or even experience to be a creative part of God's kingdom. I believe it means we are all qualified in our own way.

Praying you participate with God this week, because you are qualified . . .

---

1. Spoken at "Coffee with the Author" at St. David's Episcopal Church in Austin, Texas, October 2014.

☰ Touchstones

Initial thoughts:

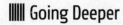 Going Deeper

How I feel called to participate in God's kingdom:

Times I have been told I wasn't "qualified:"

Unique ways I feel qualified to help to be a part of God's kingdom:

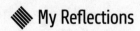 My Reflections

JANUARY

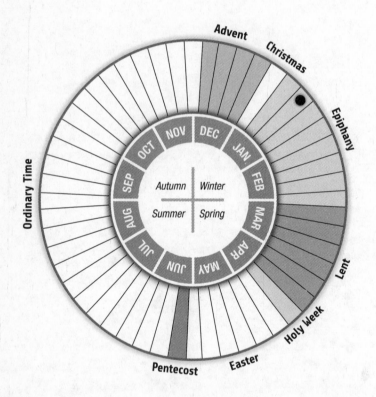

Week 3: Epiphany 2

Have you ever heard the saying: "If you can't say something nice, don't say anything at all?" It's something my mother told me. A lot! Like a lot of people, I read social media feeds, but more and more I am really surprised at some of the things people feel free to say.

Do you ever wonder if what you put out on social media or in texts ever gets misunderstood or taken the wrong way?

What about when we are face-to-face or in a group? I think sometimes we're so quick to say what we think, we don't realize how it might feel to the person we're talking to or to someone who is listening.

Consider This:

But the fruit of the Spirit is love, joy, peace, patience, kindness, goodness, faithfulness, gentleness, and self-control.

Gal. 5:22–23a

What if we could just step back and take a breath when someone says something that hurts? What if we really thought about the fruits of the Spirit and how that Spirit moves in and through us? Maybe we could offer kindness in return. And, with one kindness at a time, we could change the world.

Praying your spirit is fruitful this week . . .

≣ Touchstones

Initial thoughts:

▥ Going Deeper

Times an electronic message was misunderstood:

How I responded:

What if God read all my texts/posts?

The gifts of the Spirit that I can share:

 My Reflections

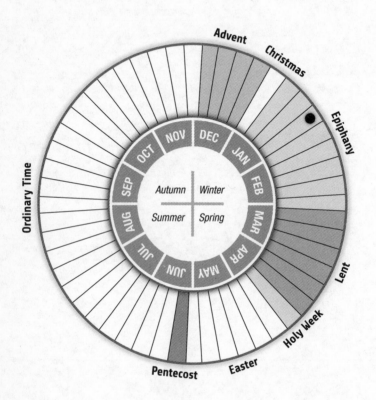

Week 4: Epiphany 3

Have you ever really trusted someone? Have you ever been hurt by a broken trust? Or, have you ever broken a trust and hurt someone?

Trust is key in close relationships like family and friendship, but it's also important in general. For example, I trust that other drivers will follow the rules of the road so that I will be safe and they expect the same from me.

I don't think, as humans, we can get along in this world without trust.

Consider This:

Although you've never seen him, you love him. Even though you don't see him now, you trust him and so rejoice with a glorious joy that is too much for words. You are receiving the goal of your faith: your salvation.

1 Pet. 1:8–9

God promises forgiveness to us no matter what. We have to trust in that. We would have no faith without trust, because trust is the foundation of our faith. Just as trust is the foundation of all relationships.

Praying you trust and are trusted this week . . .

☰ Touchstones

Initial thoughts:

||||| Going Deeper

My trust was broken when:

The forgiveness I offered, or not:

Why?

JANUARY

I broke a trust when:

How I was forgiven, or not:

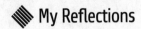 My Reflections

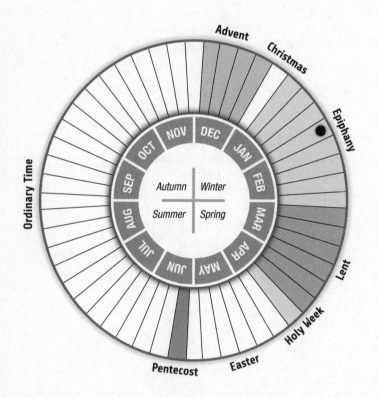

Week 5: Epiphany 4

D o you love music? When I wrote this, I lived in Austin, so for locals that might be a silly question. Music is everywhere, all the time, and I loved it! I loved walking downtown and seeing musicians on the street or being in our youth room with students singing whatever moved them at that moment.

Consider This:

Be filled with the Spirit in the following ways: speak to each other with psalms, hymns, and spiritual songs; sing and make music to the Lord in your hearts.

Eph. 5:18b–19

I have always loved music. It makes us happy and moves our feet, soothes sad feelings, and lulls babies to sleep. Music joins people together in a joyful way. It doesn't matter if you are the musician playing the instrument, the singer, or the listener enjoying it all. It's engaging and liberating; it can draw you in and set you free . . . all at the same time.

The Holy Spirit is like that: a soul-filling kind of music, soothing and joyful, engaging and liberating, drawing us in and setting us free . . . all at the same time.

Praying you have a musical week . . .

≣ Touchstones

Initial thoughts:

▐▌▌▌ Going Deeper

Things that make me feel good:

Ways I share those things with others:

How I see God in those times:

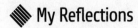 My Reflections

February

Because in the mystery of the Word made flesh, you have caused a new light to shine in our hearts, to give the knowledge of your glory in the face of your Son Jesus Christ our Lord.

Preface for Epiphany, BCP, 378

In our liturgical calendar:

- The Season of Epiphany
- Ash Wednesday and the beginning of Lent

In our secular calendar:

- February 14—Valentine's Day
- President's Day

FEBRUARY

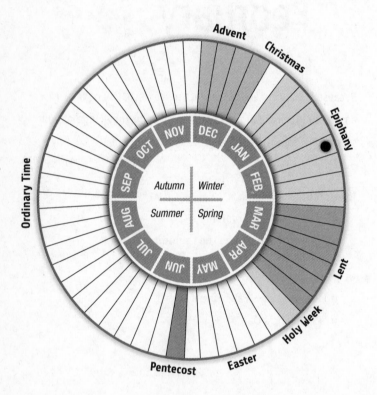

Week 6: Epiphany 5

Do you ever have bad days? It's a silly question, but think about it. Why do we have bad days? What makes them bad? Maybe your friend isn't nice, or says something mean. Maybe you have an argument with your parents. It could be you forgot to study for that big test or you didn't make the team. There are so many things that can put us in the mindset that we are having a bad day.

Consider This:

I'm convinced that nothing can separate us from God's love in Christ Jesus our Lord: not death or life, not angels or rulers, not present things or future things, not powers or height or depth, or any other thing that is created.

Rom. 8:38–39

What if we looked at our circumstances through a different lens? What if we could step back in that moment and connect to that deep abiding love that God has for us? I know that's hard—really hard, but what if we could just practice one little bit at a time? Try it with me this week. When that thing really tweaks your nerves, take a deep breath and just feel God's love. It's always there for you. Don't let your circumstances dictate your joy or happiness. Let God do that . . .

Praying your "tweaks" become joys this week . . .

≣ Touchstones

Initial thoughts:

▦ Going Deeper

Things that make a day bad for me:

How I react to them:

How I react to the people around me:

How I can look at those circumstances differently:

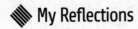 My Reflections

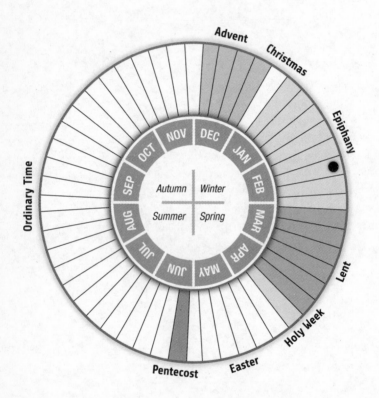

Week 7: Valentine's Day
(Epiphany 6)

February 14th is the day most people in many areas around the world celebrate Valentine's Day. A day where we buy cards, candy, and flowers for the ones we love. There are so many songs, poems, and stories written about love and all its many forms.

Consider This:

Love is patient, love is kind, it isn't jealous, it doesn't brag, it isn't arrogant; it isn't rude, it doesn't seek its own advantage, it isn't irritable, it doesn't keep a record of complaints, it isn't happy with injustice, but it is happy with the truth. Love puts up with all things, trusts in all things, hopes for all things, endures all things. Love never fails.

1 Cor. 13:4–8a

This is a passage often read at weddings. On the surface it looks like it would fit right in on a Valentine's Day card, but I think it's deeper. Jesus has a deep abiding love for us that endures all things. Jesus is an example to us of how to love without making it about ourselves; an unselfish love. What if our love for another had no conditions? What if we could learn to love people right where they are, how they are? What if we could really love like Jesus?

Praying you experience unconditional love this week . . .

≡ Touchstones

Initial thoughts:

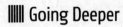 Going Deeper

Ways I want to be loved:

Ways I can put myself aside:

Ways I can show others Jesus's love:

Ways I can receive God's love for me:

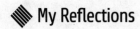 My Reflections

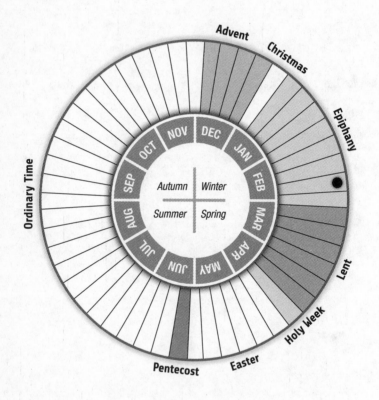

Week 8: Epiphany 7

This Little Light of Mine is one of my favorite childhood songs. I love sharing it with really small children and getting them to yell, "No!" at the right time of the song. It is fun to watch them get such a kick out of yelling! But what are they yelling about?

Consider This:

In the same way, let your light shine before people, so they can see the good things you do and praise your Father who is in heaven.

Matt. 5:16

and this:

No one lights a lamp and then covers it with a bowl or puts it under a bed. Instead, they put it on top of a lampstand so that those who enter can see the light.

Luke 8:16

Are we singing about Jesus as the light? Are we singing about the light within us? Is Jesus the light within us? I think "yes" to all of the above. Jesus said people must become like little children to enter the kingdom of heaven. So what if we really did? What if we became like little children joyfully shouting loudly that no one was going to hide our light under a bushel? What if we became like little children gleefully letting our little light shine?

Praying your light shines brightly this week . . .

≣ Touchstones

Initial thoughts:

|||| Going Deeper

Ways I hide my light under a "bushel":

Ways I shine my light:

Things that make that decision for me:

Time when I'm afraid to shine but wish I could:

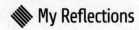 My Reflections

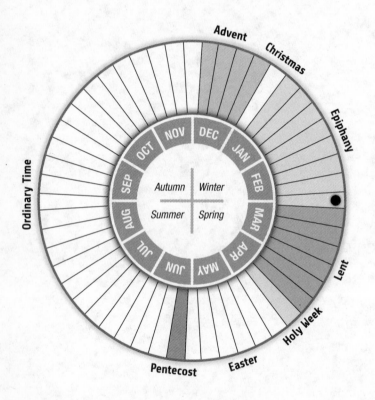

Week 9: Epiphany 8

"Be yourself, everyone else is already taken," said Oscar Wilde. Be yourself. It sounds simple, but I think it can be really hard sometimes. What does that even mean? Be yourself. How do we figure out who we are? We get lots of messages from a multitude of directions telling us what we should be, how we should look, what we should wear, what we should drive. How do we know?

Consider This:

God created humanity in God's own image, in the divine image God created them, male and female God created them.

Gen. 1:27

God created you. God created me. We are different, yet bound together by the same Holy Spirit. You and I don't look alike, yet inside there is a familiarity. I think we get that confused with the outside. The body is temporary. It will age and get wrinkled, but the inside will continue to grow, bloom, and seek a connection with the divine. You are beautiful, holy, and created in God's own image. Be yourself, everyone else is already taken.

Praying you see God's beauty in the mirror this week . . .

☰ Touchstones

Initial thoughts:

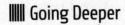 # Going Deeper

Who I think I am:

How I try to be like others:

What I feel when I recognize myself as made in God's image:

Ways I can help others see God's beauty in them:

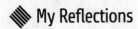 My Reflections

March

Through Jesus Christ our Lord. For our sins he was lifted high upon the cross, that he might draw the whole world to himself; and, by his suffering and death, he became the source of eternal salvation for all who put their trust in him.

Preface for the Season of Lent, BCP, 379

In our liturgical calendar:

- Sometimes Ash Wednesday
- The Season of Lent
- Sometimes Holy Week and Easter

In our secular calendar:

- March 20 or 21—Vernal (Spring) Equinox
- Spring break

MARCH

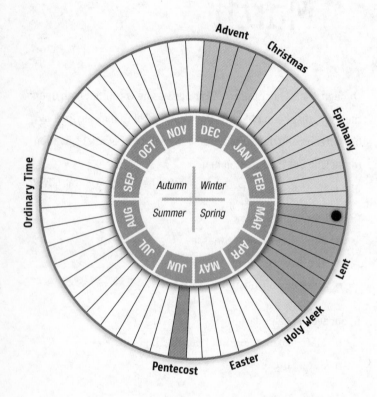

Ash Wednesday

Stuff. . . . I think in general, most people have a lot of stuff.
I do. Things we don't really need, but keep anyway; thinking
it might come in handy one day. We buy things that we don't
need simply because we want them. We collect things and we
treasure them. It's not necessarily bad to have lots of stuff, but is
it getting in the way of something else? Could it be that we focus
on the tangibles around us and thereby forget the intangibles?

Consider This:

*Stop collecting treasures for your own benefit on earth, where moth
and rust eat them and where thieves break in and steal them. Instead,
collect treasures for yourselves in heaven, where moth and rust don't
eat them and where thieves don't break in and steal them. Where
your treasure is, there your heart will be also.*

Matt. 6:19–21

Lent is a time of reflection, prayer, fasting, self-denial, spiritual
growth, almsgiving, and simplicity. Begin your Lent by looking
around at your "treasures." What do you really need . . . really?
Consider sharing your treasures. What could you give to a shel-
ter? What items might you be willing to part with so that others
may have?

Praying for your heavenly treasures . . .

My thoughts and prayers as I begin my Lenten journey:

My Lenten observance (What I might give up or take on):

≡ Touchstones

Initial thoughts:

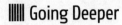 Going Deeper

What are my earthly treasures?

Why are they so important to me?

What can I let go?

Where is God in all the "stuff" of my life?

 My Reflections

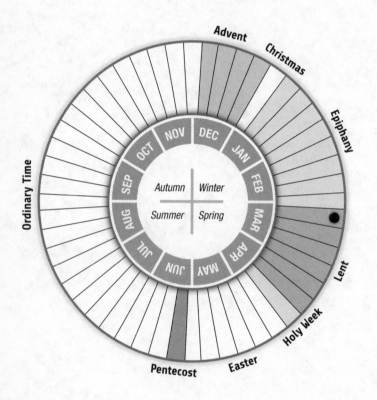

Week 10: Lent 1

The beginning of Lent, for me, is one of those times of both/
and. I am both excited and nervous, looking forward to it and
dreading it all at the same time. It reminds me of the first day
of kindergarten—children looking so forward to going to school
and yet scared at the same time; parents excited for the new
chapter, assuring us "I love you" and then sending us into the
unknown.

Consider This:

In those days Jesus came from Nazareth of Galilee and was bap-
tized by John in the Jordan. And just as he was coming up out of the
water, he saw the heavens torn apart and the Spirit descending like
a dove on him. And a voice came from heaven, "You are my Son, the
Beloved; with you I am well pleased." And the Spirit immediately
drove him out into the wilderness. He was in the wilderness forty
days, tempted by Satan; and he was with the wild beasts; and the
angels waited on him.

Mark 1:9–13

As we enter into the unknown, the wilderness, let us keep in mind
that we are the beloved with whom God is well pleased. There is
nothing we can do to drive God from us—we are the only ones
that stand in the way of receiving love as the Beloved. God loves
us and then sends us out into the unknown. It is up to us to go.

Praying you know God's love as you enter the wilderness . . .

≡ Touchstones

Initial thoughts:

My prayer:

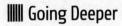 ## Going Deeper

Times I have been in the wilderness:

The love that brought me out of the wilderness:

Where I see God in the challenges of my life:

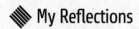 My Reflections

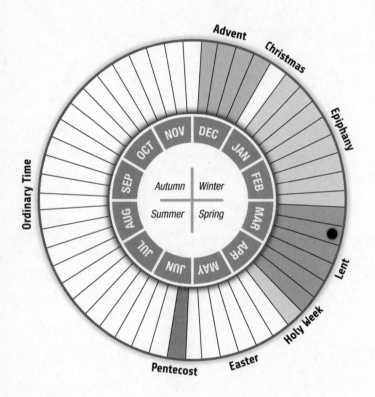

Week 11: Lent 2

Have you ever fasted? On purpose? There are many times that I skip a meal, but I assure you, it is not on purpose. Several faith traditions call for fasting at some time during their seasons, celebrations, and remembrances. We are called to fast at times as well, especially during Lent.

Consider This:

And when you fast, don't put on a sad face like the hypocrites. They distort their faces so people will know they are fasting. I assure you that they have their reward. When you fast, brush your hair and wash your face.

Matt. 6:16–17

I am one of those people for whom fasting is hard. But it also really makes me think of the challenges that many people face, including the lack of nutritious food. There is such an abundance of food in our community and so many that are hungry. What if for just one day we packed a nice lunch, but instead of having it ourselves, we simply gave it away? There are so many opportunities for "random acts of kindness"—giving away our lunch is just one. What can you do in secret today?

Praying you can share an anonymous gift today . . .

 Touchstones

Initial thoughts:

My prayer:

|||| Going Deeper

My fast (If not food, or a food item, what will I give up?):

What is keeping me from growing closer to God?

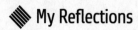 My Reflections

MARCH

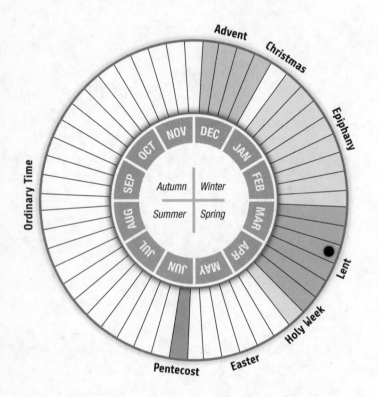

Week 12: Lent 3

What is prayer? Sometimes I think it can feel a little intimidating. What if I do it wrong? Is there something I should say each time? Is there a right place? When am I supposed to pray? If nothing is going wrong, should I still pray? What do I pray for?

Consider This:

Early in the morning, well before sunrise, Jesus rose and went to a deserted place where he could be alone in prayer.

Mark 1:35

Prayer is a little word that carries a big impact. I don't believe there is a wrong way to pray, but I do believe that God waits patiently for us to come to that place where we cannot do anything without prayer. That takes practice—a lifetime of practice. We read over and over again in the Bible where Jesus would regularly go off alone to pray. It is in that time and space that we come into the presence of a God that loves us no matter what. Always abiding . . . always loving. Give yourself the gift of prayer. Find your time of day and go alone to pray and be with God.

Praying you find time to be alone with God . . .

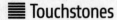 Touchstones

Initial thoughts:

My prayer:

 Going Deeper

Times in my life for prayer:

Times in my daily schedule for prayer:

MARCH

What's stopping me?

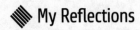 My Reflections

MARCH

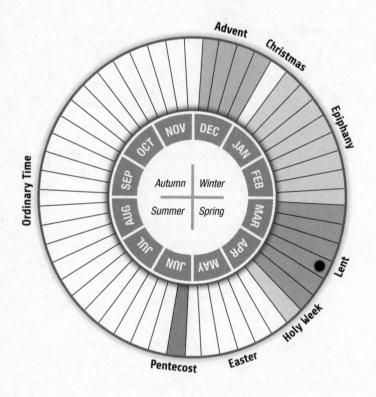

Week 13: Lent 4

Temptation. Have you ever been tempted? Of course there are small temptations around us all the time: having that extra dessert, hitting the snooze on the alarm clock a couple more times, postponing working on that one assignment or project, speeding through a yellow light, and the list goes on.

Temptation is a constant thing in our lives. We can think about Jesus in the wilderness for forty days being tempted by Satan or we can think about it in terms of the small day-to-day choices we make—especially when we're tempted to make a decision that might not be the best.

Consider This:

Forgive us for the ways we have wronged you, just as we also forgive those who have wronged us. And don't lead us into temptation, but rescue us from the evil one.

Matt. 6:12–13

I notice in the Lord's Prayer that Jesus teaches us to pray by asking for forgiveness first and then clearly expects us to offer that same forgiveness to others. Only then are we guided to ask to be lead away from temptation. The hard part about that is that God knows we are going to wrong someone, that we are going to make mistakes and need forgiveness. At the same time, it is in God's grace that we are already forgiven, even when we do give in to temptation.

Praying you accept forgiveness from temptation this week . . .

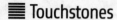 Touchstones

Initial thoughts:

My prayer:

▓ Going Deeper

Times I've been tempted and resisted:

Times I've been tempted . . . and gave in:

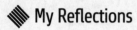 My Reflections

April

But chiefly are we bound to praise you for the glorious resurrection of your Son Jesus Christ our Lord; for he is the true Pascal Lamb, who was sacrificed for us, and has taken away the sin of the world. By his death he has destroyed death, and by his rising to life again he has won for us everlasting life.

Preface for Easter Season, BCP, 379

In our liturgical calendar:

- Often Holy Week and Easter
- The Season of Easter
- Sometimes Pentecost

In our secular calendar:

- April 1—April Fool's Day
- April 15—Tax Day
- April 22—Earth Day

APRIL

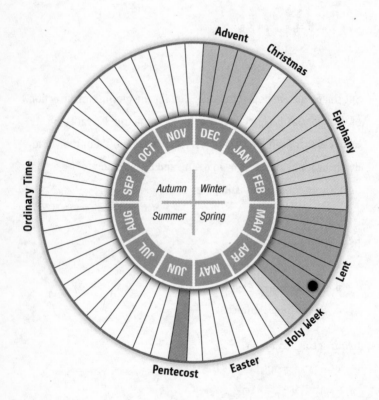

Week 14: Lent 5

Sin. We don't like to talk about sin. It's messy and uncomfortable, but it's true. We are all sinners. We do the wrong thing, make the wrong decision, avoid the truth or completely lie, say the wrong thing and cause hurt to another, and so on. Life is hard and we are sinners. But there is Good News. . . .

Consider This:

Or what woman, if she owns ten silver coins and loses one of them, won't light a lamp and sweep the house, searching her home carefully until she finds it? When she finds it, she calls together her friends and neighbors, saying, "Celebrate with me because I've found my lost coin." In the same way, I tell you, joy breaks out in the presence of God's angels over one sinner who changes both heart and life.

Luke 15:8–10

Every time we sin, and ask for forgiveness, we are forgiven. By our baptism we are forgiven and receive the gift of the Holy Spirit. It is a joyful and lighthearted feeling to think of the angels breaking out in a celebration when I acknowledge my own weakness. What will you do to change your "heart and life"?

Praying you feel the heavenly celebrations this week . . .

≡ Touchstones

Initial thoughts:

My prayer:

▥ Going Deeper

My weaknesses:

Public (the ones people can see):

Private (the ones no one knows about):

Where does my heart need to be changed?

 My Reflections

APRIL

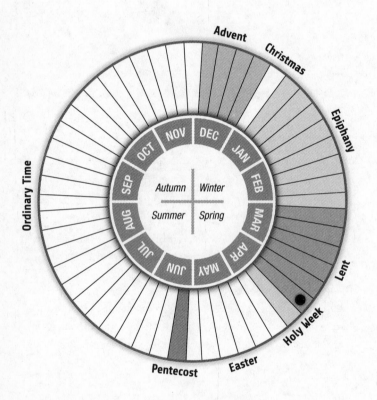

Week 15: Preparing for Holy Week (*Lent 6*)

Holy Week . . . it's the time in the church year when we begin the week on a high note reading about the celebration of Jesus coming to Jerusalem with palm branches being laid before him as jubilant voices sing, "Hosanna! Blessings on the one who comes in the name of the Lord!" Only to have the week take a dark turn after the Last Supper when Jesus is arrested and subsequently crucified, dies, and is buried. The weekend feels really long, and then there is the glorious celebration of Jesus's resurrection!

Have you ever had a time in your life where your emotions were high and low, and then high again because of events out of your control? A time when you felt things were going great only to have everything fall apart, but in the end, it was even better than before?

This is our story. We are Easter people. We are always being born anew. There is forever the promise of a new beginning; a fresh start. We are never so far down the wrong path that we can't turn around and know God will be there for us: ever patient, ever loving, ever present.

I invite you into the Passion story with daily readings this week. Be intentional with your time so you can wonder, ponder, feel, digest.

Before each reading, offer your time to God and invite the Holy Spirit to be present with you. At the end of each reading, offer a prayer of thanksgiving in whatever way you feel called.

≡ Touchstones

Initial thoughts:

My prayer for Holy Week:

IIIII Going Deeper

Reflections on my Lenten journey so far:

How I feel going into Holy Week:

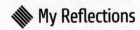 My Reflections

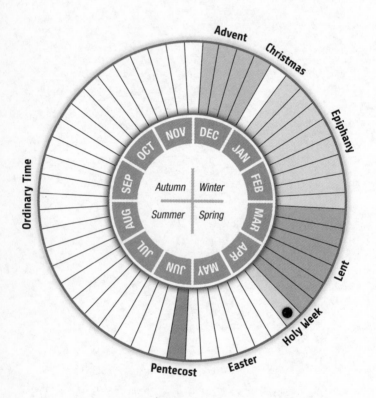

Week 16: Palm Sunday

Entry into Jerusalem

Now a large crowd spread their clothes on the road. Others cut palm branches off the trees and spread them on the road. The crowds in front of him and behind him shouted, "Hosanna to the Son of David! Blessings on the one who comes in the name of the Lord! Hosanna in the highest!" And when Jesus entered Jerusalem, the whole city was stirred up. "Who is this?" they asked. The crowds answered, "It's the prophet Jesus from Nazareth in Galilee."

Matt. 21:8–11

≡ Touchstones

Initial thoughts:

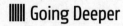 Going Deeper

Prayer for today:

Prayer for tomorrow:

 My Reflections

Monday in Holy Week

The Last Supper

While they were eating, Jesus took bread, blessed it, broke it, and gave it to the disciples and said, "Take and eat. This is my body." He took a cup, gave thanks, and gave it to them, saying, "Drink from this, all of you. This is my blood of the covenant, which is poured out for many so that their sins may be forgiven. I tell you, I won't drink wine again until that day when I drink it in a new way with you in my Father's kingdom."

Matt. 26:26–29

≡ Touchstones

Initial thoughts:

||||| Going Deeper

My thoughts on what it might have been like at the Last Supper:

My thoughts about Holy Communion:

My prayer:

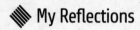 My Reflections

Tuesday in Holy Week

Jesus's Arrest

While Jesus was still speaking, Judas, one of the Twelve, came. With him was a large crowd carrying swords and clubs. They had been sent by the chief priests and elders of the people. His betrayer had given them a sign: "Arrest the man I kiss." Just then he came to Jesus and said, "Hello, Rabbi." Then he kissed him. But Jesus said to him, "Friend, do what you came to do." Then they came and grabbed Jesus and arrested him. One of those with Jesus reached for his sword. Striking the high priest's slave, he cut off his ear. Then Jesus said to him, "Put the sword back into its place. All those who use the sword will die by the sword. Or do you think that I'm not able to ask my Father and he will send to me more than twelve battle groups of angels right away? But if I did that, how would the scriptures be fulfilled that say this must happen?" Then Jesus said to the crowds, "Have you come with swords and clubs to arrest me, like a thief? Day after day, I sat in the temple teaching, but you didn't arrest me. But all this has happened so that what the prophets said in the scriptures might be fulfilled." Then all the disciples left Jesus and ran away.

Matt. 26:47–56

≣ Touchstones

Initial thoughts:

▌▌▌▌ Going Deeper

How does it feel to be wrongly accused?

My prayer for those wrongly accused:

My prayer:

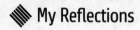 My Reflections

Wednesday in Holy Week

Peter's Denial

Meanwhile, Peter was sitting outside in the courtyard. A servant woman came and said to him, "You were also with Jesus the Galilean." But he denied it in front of all of them, saying, "I don't know what you are talking about." When he went over to the gate, another woman saw him and said to those who were there, "This man was with Jesus, the man from Nazareth." With a solemn pledge, he denied it again, saying, "I don't know the man." A short time later those standing there came and said to Peter, "You must be one of them. The way you talk gives you away." Then he cursed and swore, "I don't know the man!" At that very moment the rooster crowed. Peter remembered Jesus' words, "Before the rooster crows you will deny me three times." And Peter went out and cried uncontrollably.

Matt. 26:69–75

≣ Touchstones

Initial thoughts:

▒ Going Deeper

Times a friend has "denied" me:

How I reacted:

My prayer:

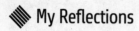 My Reflections

Thursday in Holy Week

The Crucifixion

Pilate said, "Then what should I do with Jesus who is called Christ?"
They all said, "Crucify him!" But he said, "Why? What wrong has he
done?" They shouted even louder, "Crucify him!"

As they were going out, they found Simon, a man from Cyrene.
They forced him to carry his cross. When they came to a place called
Golgotha, which means Skull Place, they gave Jesus wine mixed
with vinegar to drink. But after tasting it, he didn't want to drink it.
After they crucified him, they divided up his clothes among them by
drawing lots. They sat there, guarding him. They placed above his
head the charge against him. It read, "This is Jesus, the king of the
Jews." They crucified with him two outlaws, one on his right side and
one on his left. Those who were walking by insulted Jesus, shaking
their heads and saying, "So you were going to destroy the temple
and rebuild it in three days, were you? Save yourself! If you are God's
Son, come down from the cross." In the same way, the chief priests,
along with the legal experts and the elders, were making fun of him,
saying, "He saved others, but he can't save himself. He's the king of
Israel, so let him come down from the cross now. Then we'll believe
in him. He trusts in God, so let God deliver him now if he wants to.
He said, 'I'm God's Son.'" The outlaws who were crucified with him
insulted him in the same way.

Matt. 27:22–23, 32–44

≡ Touchstones

Initial thoughts:

▥ Going Deeper

Pontius Pilate goes along with the crowd and orders Jesus to be crucified. He clearly doesn't think Jesus has done anything wrong.

Time(s) when I have "gone along with the crowd" because I was afraid to go against them:

My prayer:

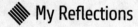

My Reflections

Friday in Holy Week

Jesus's Death

From noon until three in the afternoon the whole earth was dark. At about three Jesus cried out with a loud shout, "Eli, Eli, lama sabach-thani," which means, "My God, my God, why have you left me?" After hearing him, some standing there said, "He's calling Elijah." One of them ran over, took a sponge full of vinegar, and put it on a pole. He offered it to Jesus to drink. But the rest of them said, "Let's see if Elijah will come and save him." Again Jesus cried out with a loud shout. Then he died. Look, the curtain of the sanctuary was torn in two from top to bottom. The earth shook, the rocks split, and the bodies of many holy people who had died were raised. After Jesus' resurrection they came out of their graves and went into the holy city where they appeared to many people. When the centurion and those with him who were guarding Jesus saw the earthquake and what had just happened, they were filled with awe and said, "This was certainly God's Son."

Matt. 27:45–54

≣ Touchstones

Initial thoughts:

IIIII Going Deeper

Jesus cries out, "My God, my God, why have you left me?"

Time(s) when I feel God has left me:

Time(s) I knew God was with me:

My prayer:

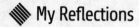 My Reflections

Saturday in Holy Week

Jesus's Burial

That evening a man named Joseph came. He was a rich man from Arimathea who had become a disciple of Jesus. He came to Pilate and asked for Jesus' body. Pilate gave him permission to take it. Joseph took the body, wrapped it in a clean linen cloth, and laid it in his own new tomb, which he had carved out of the rock. After he rolled a large stone at the door of the tomb, he went away. Mary Magdalene and the other Mary were there, sitting in front of the tomb. The next day, which was the day after Preparation Day, the chief priests and the Pharisees gathered before Pilate. They said, "Sir, we remember that while that deceiver was still alive he said, 'After three days I will arise.' Therefore, order the grave to be sealed until the third day. Otherwise, his disciples may come and steal the body and tell the people, 'He's been raised from the dead.' This last deception will be worse than the first." Pilate replied, "You have soldiers for guard duty. Go and make it as secure as you know how." Then they went and secured the tomb by sealing the stone and posting the guard.

Matt. 27:57–66

≣ Touchstones

Initial thoughts:

▒ Going Deeper

How I feel about Jesus's death:

APRIL

Prayer for those who have died:

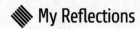 My Reflections

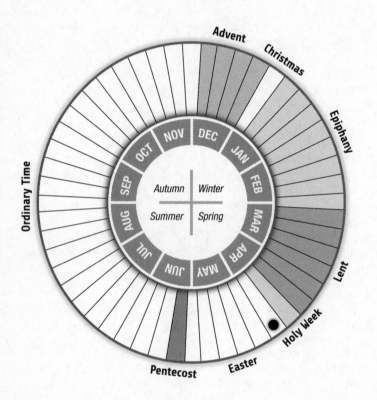

Week 17: Easter Sunday

The Resurrection: The Lord Is Risen Indeed!

After the Sabbath, at dawn on the first day of the week, Mary Magdalene and the other Mary came to look at the tomb. Look, there was a great earthquake, for an angel from the Lord came down from heaven. Coming to the stone, he rolled it away and sat on it. Now his face was like lightning and his clothes as white as snow. The guards were so terrified of him that they shook with fear and became like dead men. But the angel said to the women, "Don't be afraid. I know that you are looking for Jesus who was crucified. He isn't here, because he's been raised from the dead, just as he said. Come, see the place where they laid him. Now hurry, go and tell his disciples, 'He's been raised from the dead. He's going on ahead of you to Galilee. You will see him there.'"

Matt. 28:1–7a

≣ Touchstones

Initial thoughts:

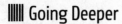 Going Deeper

My prayers of joy! Hallelujah!

How I will go forward out of Lent and into Easter, being resurrected with Jesus by the Holy Spirit?

APRIL

How I have been renewed:

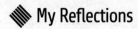

My Reflections

APRIL

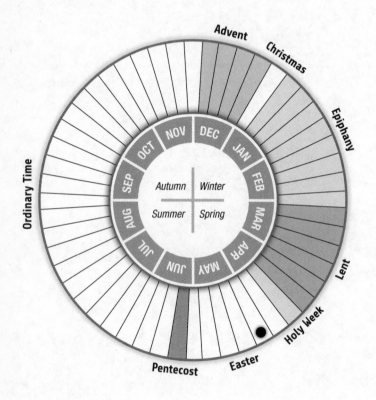

Week 18: Easter 2

Endurance is an interesting word. If you are an athlete, having endurance is a good thing. You can run farther, play longer, and outlast your opponent. If you are having trouble at school, with your friends, family, or other relationships, then endurance or having to endure is not such a good thing.

Consider This:

Look at how we honor those who have practiced endurance. You have heard of the endurance of Job. And you have seen what the Lord has accomplished, for the Lord is full of compassion and mercy.

James 5:11

Job is always the example of how to endure the worst situations with faith, but none of us want to be him! The storms of life will come in a variety of forms and severity, but in them all, God is there with you. It is sometimes hard to know or to see or to even believe, but it is true. God is there with you; holding you as a beloved child and helping you to endure when you alone cannot.

Praying you feel God's enduring love this week . . .

≣ Touchstones

Initial thoughts:

||||| Going Deeper

My struggles:

How I endure them:

How I invite God into them:

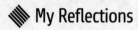 My Reflections

May

We give you thanks, most gracious God, for the beauty of earth and sky and sea; for the richness of mountains, plains, and rivers; for the songs of birds and loveliness of flowers. We praise you for these good gifts, and pray that we may safeguard them for our posterity. Grant that we may continue to grow in our grateful enjoyment of your abundant creation, to the honor and glory of your Name, now and for ever. Amen.

Prayer for the Beauty of the Earth, BCP, 840

In our liturgical calendar:

- Ascension Day
- Pentecost

In our secular calendar:

- 2nd Sunday in May—Mother's Day
- Last Monday in May—Memorial Day

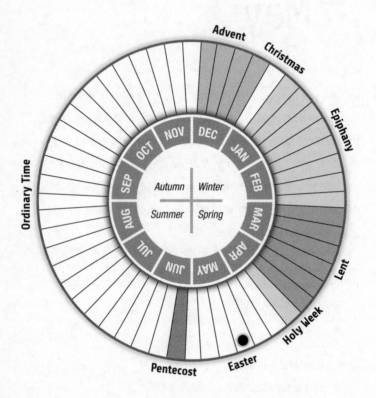

Week 19: Easter 3

Have you ever heard the term "spring fever?" It's an actual thing. Wikipedia puts it like this: "It is a term applied to several sets of physical and psychological symptoms associated with the arrival of spring."[2] It's that feeling you get when the sun is warm, the air is clear, and you want to be anywhere other than where you are. The winter that was long, cold, wet, and windy is over. Now it's beautiful and you just want to be outside!

Consider This:

So then, if anyone is in Christ, that person is part of the new creation. The old things have gone away, and look, new things have arrived!

2 Cor. 5:17

Easter is like that for me. Lent is long and dark and seems to go on forever. But then it's Easter and with it all new things; bright flowers and people smiling and family together.

Our lives can also have seasons that are long and dark and seem to go on forever. But then the light begins to seep in; slowly at first like the breaking dawn. And then more and more until one day we feel better—lighter somehow. When we look back, we see how dark things were; we know we are now on the healing side where old things have gone away and new things have arrived.

Praying for you that the old has gone and the new has arrived . . .

---

2. Wikipedia, s.v. "Spring Fever," last modified January 7, 2015, https://en.wikipedia.org/wiki/Spring_fever.

≡ Touchstones

Initial thoughts:

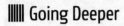 Going Deeper

The dark season(s) of my life have been:

I know God was at work in my life because . . .

I feel like I am "new" when . . .

I get my own "spring fever" feeling when . . .

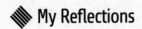 My Reflections

MAY

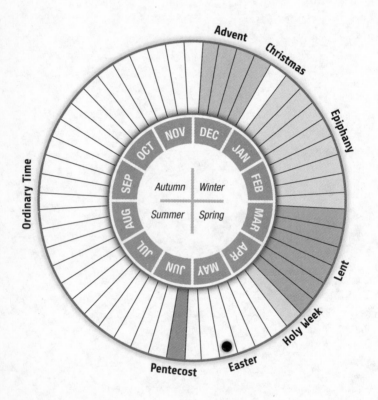

Week 20: Easter 4

"People think I'm just _____." Have you ever had that thought cross your mind? You could fill in that blank with anything on any given day. "People think I'm just a smart kid" or "People think I'm mean because I don't talk." It's so easy for people to think they know us or make assumptions that are wrong because they haven't taken the time to get to know us. They might judge us because we don't talk much or because we talk too much. We might be judged because we never smile or because we smile too much. The list can go on and on.

Consider This:

"The reason the world does not know us is that it did not know him. Dear friends, now we are children of God, and what we will be has not yet been made known."

1 John 3:1b–2a NIV

Jesus experienced much of that same phenomenon. People around him judged him based on any number of things because they never took the time to get to know him. What if we decided to do things differently? What if we withheld judgment, waiting just to know someone? What if we didn't pay attention to the fact that they don't make eye contact or smile? What if we fully paid attention to each person for who they really are? For the person inside that wants to be known, the person that wants to be loved and accepted? What if we did it differently?

Praying you take the time to get to know someone in a new way this week . . .

≣ Touchstones

Initial thoughts:

||||| Going Deeper

Who I am:

I am afraid to let people know me better because:

What I wish people knew about me:

Things I can do to be genuinely who God made me to be:

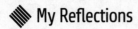 My Reflections

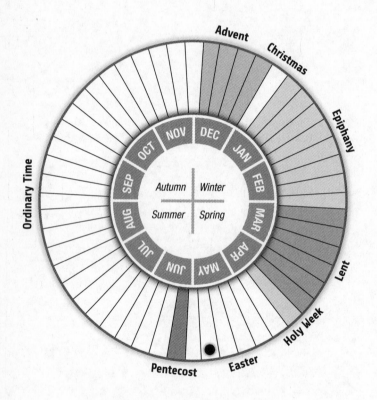

Week 21: Exam Time (*Easter 5*)

The school year is coming quickly to a close. It's that time of year when the weather warms up, the shorts and sandals come out, and we can see the end of school so clearly! It's almost summer, with time for vacations, camp, and friends . . . but first—exams. It causes such stress . . . but why? Is it expected that you should stress over it? We lose so much time worrying! Have you ever noticed what you miss when you're so consumed with worry?

Consider This:

You who are young, make the most of your youth. Relish your youthful vigor. Follow the impulses of your heart. If something looks good to you, pursue it. But know also that not just anything goes; You have to answer to God for every last bit of it. Live footloose and fancy-free— you won't be young forever. Youth lasts about as long as smoke."

Eccles. 11:9–10 The Message

Being young is hard sometimes; much harder than it really should be. Society wants you to have your life planned out and to have a complete resume built by the time you're 14 . . . and even that's late! Don't misunderstand. It is good to do your best. *Your* best. not someone else's idea of what your best is. What would it be like to do your best just for you, to fully enjoy and experience life as it unfolds? What would it be like to really just be you . . . the person God created you to be?

Praying you enjoy playing outside this week . . .

≡ Touchstones

Initial thoughts:

||||| Going Deeper

My biggest worry right now is:

My prayer for helping to put this aside:

Some steps I know I can take to help me feel more at peace:

People who I can ask for help:

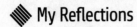 My Reflections

MAY

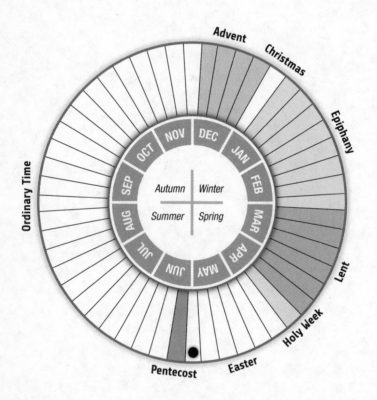

Week 22: For Memorial Day
(Easter 6)

Memorial Day brings around a variety of thoughts. What do you think about? School is coming to a close, seasons are changing, and we begin to look to summer. Memorial Day has become the turning point, or kickoff, of summertime and all the activities that go with it. And those things are so much fun!

Consider This:

This is how we know love: Jesus laid down his life for us, and we ought to lay down our lives for our brothers and sisters.

1 John 3:16

Memorial Day was originally called "Decoration Day" after the Civil War. It was established as a time for the nation to flower, or decorate, the graves of those who died in war. In more recent times it has been extended to honor all Americans who have died while in military service.

Our servicemen and -women lay down their lives for us every day without thought or concern of the politics that surround them. They train, study, and engage in practices that keep them focused.

Jesus laid down his life without thought or concern of the politics that surrounded him daily. He prayed, studied, and engaged in practices that kept him focused.

I'm not suggesting that we should not enjoy friends, family, and the hot dog on the grill on Memorial Day as we look forward to the days of summer. I am suggesting that there is always time for us to pray, study, and engage in practices that will keep our spirits close to God.

Praying for you a calm summer breeze . . .

≣ Touchstones

Initial thoughts:

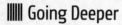 Going Deeper

What Memorial Day means to me:

Ways my family celebrates together:

Practices I can engage in to help my faith grow:

Ways I can share those practices with others:

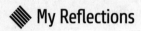 My Reflections

June

O God, our heavenly Father, whose glory fills the whole creation, and whose presence we find wherever we go: Preserve those who travel; surround them with your loving care; protect them from every danger; and bring them in safety to their journey's end; through Jesus Christ our Lord. Amen.

A Prayer for Travelers, BCP, 831

In our liturgical calendar:

- Sometimes Pentecost
- The Season after Pentecost (Ordinary Time)

In our secular calendar:

- June 14—Flag Day
- 3rd Sunday in June—Father's Day
- June 20–22—Summer Solstice
- Final exams & end of the school year
- Vacations, summer camps, mission trips

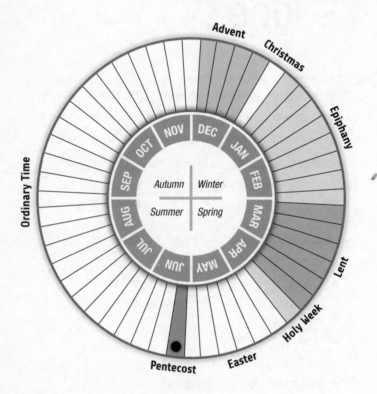

Week 23: Pentecost

Do you speak more than one language? I can understand and read more of other languages than I can actually speak. Language is fascinating to me in its complexity: its ability to comfort or hurt, to instruct and guide. But just because we speak the same language doesn't always mean we understand each other.

Consider This:

When Pentecost Day arrived, they were all together in one place. Suddenly a sound from heaven like the howling of a fierce wind filled the entire house where they were sitting. They saw what seemed to be individual flames of fire alighting on each one of them. They were all filled with the Holy Spirit and began to speak in other languages as the Spirit enabled them to speak.

Acts 2:1–4

What would happen if we allowed the Holy Spirit to guide our language? What if we were to seek first to understand someone instead of trying to be understood? What if we used our language to comfort each other in times of need and encourage each other in times of trial? What if we used our language to lift up, celebrate, and proclaim that God is good?

Praying you feel a deeper understanding this week . . .

≣ Touchstones

Initial thoughts:

||||| Going Deeper

Ways I can better use my language:

Ways I lift up and support my friends and family:

Ways I could do that better:

Ways I celebrate God with my words:

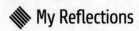 My Reflections

JUNE

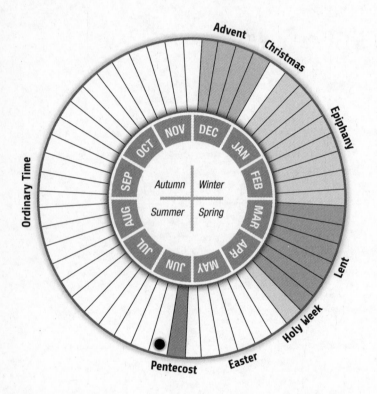

Week 24: Summer
(Ordinary Time)

Summer break . . . it's such a relief! No more homework, books, notes, or projects! It is time to take a deep breath and then decide what we're going to do for the next few months. It's officially time to play!

Consider This:

Sing to him a new song! Play your best with joyful shouts!

Ps. 33:3

There are a lot of instructions for us in Scripture. Lots! I think many times we overlook the really fun ones and go for the deep, instructional ones that help us with rules and guidelines for our lives, and that's good, really good. But what about the fun ones? What about the ones that remind us to be like children and to dance and to play, to live and sing and make a joyful noise?

Praying you find time to play this week . . .

≣ Touchstones

Initial thoughts:

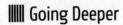 Going Deeper

"Play" to me means:

How I feel when I really play, like when I was a small child:

How I see God in playtime:

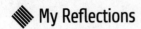 My Reflections

JUNE

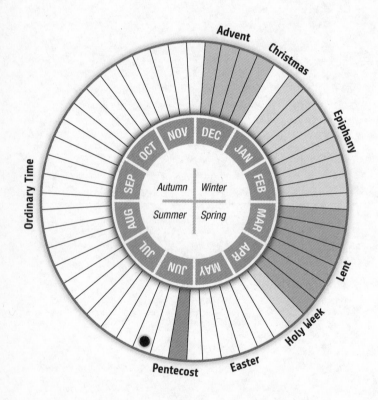

Week 25: Summer (Ordinary Time)

Mission trips are the source of some of my best summer memories. Some of them have been in the town where I live, some as far away as another country—and everywhere in between. The jobs have varied from weeding a vegetable garden to reroofing a home. None of those jobs were any more or less important or impactful than the next. Why?

Consider This:

We have different gifts that are consistent with God's grace that has been given to us. If your gift is prophecy, you should prophesy in proportion to your faith. If your gift is service, devote yourself to serving. If your gift is teaching, devote yourself to teaching. If your gift is encouragement, devote yourself to encouraging. The one giving should do it with no strings attached. The leader should lead with passion. The one showing mercy should be cheerful.

Rom. 12:6–8

Sometimes I think we feel like the bigger the job, the more visible our final product is, the better work we did! Not true. Everyone has a different gift and should use it accordingly. If babysitting is your gift, offer some free time to your neighborhood moms. If gardening is your gift, offer to help a community garden. No strings attached. Just do it because you can. You will be honoring God by using that gift you have that is uniquely yours.

Praying you use your gifts with no strings attached this week . . .

≣ Touchstones

Initial thoughts:

⦀ Going Deeper

My gifts:

How I use them:

What strings are attached:

How I can let go of those strings:

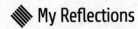 My Reflections

JUNE

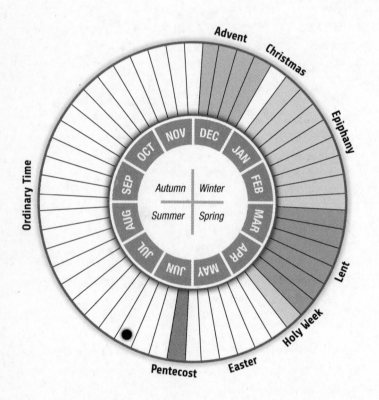

Week 26: Summer
(Ordinary Time)

Summer isn't usually one of those times when people think about "new" things in nature. That's kind of a spring thing, but then I think about the cicada. I always know it is summer when I hear the cicadas. The ones you hear are not very pretty to look at. They are a brown beetle-like bug. You usually find the empty shell stuck to trees. But the cicada is the perfect example of how we can be new creations in Christ. After years of living underground in the dark, the cicada comes out into the light and works really hard to break out of its shell. The emerging insect is really beautiful.

Consider This:

So then, if anyone is in Christ, that person is part of the new creation. The old things have gone away, and look, new things have arrived!

2 Cor. 5:17

What would it be like if we could really shed our hard outer shell? To really let out that inner beauty that God has created in us to share with the world? What if we truly embraced the love God has for us, just as we are, and shared that with those around us? It's not easy, breaking out of that shell, but what emerges is beautiful.

Praying you can break out of that shell this week . . .

≡ Touchstones

Initial thoughts:

▦ Going Deeper

Things that keep me inside my shell:

What it would feel like to shed it:

Ways I can allow God to help:

Ways I can let my inner beauty out:

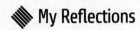 My Reflections

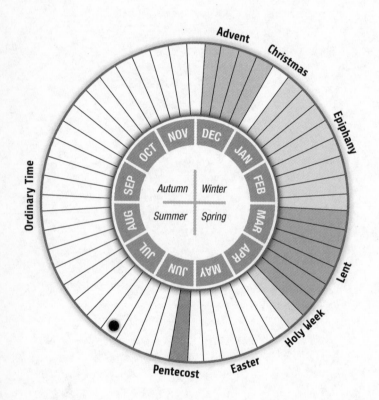

Week 27: Summer (Ordinary Time)

Have you ever heard of or played the game *SORRY!?* It's a popular one at our house. Have you ever noticed the tag line? "The game of sweet revenge." Wow! I never noticed that before. We groan when we get sent back to "home" and cheer when we get to put someone else farther behind in the game. It really is a game about "getting even" with someone for a wrong done all in the attempt to win.

Consider This:

He committed no sin, nor did he ever speak in ways meant to deceive. When he was insulted, he did not reply with insults. When he suffered, he did not threaten revenge. Instead, he entrusted himself to the one who judges justly. He carried in his own body on the cross the sins we committed. He did this so that we might live in righteousness, having nothing to do with sin. By his wounds you were healed.

1 Pet. 2:22–24

When we get hurt in life, or are insulted or wronged, we want justice and we want it now! We want that person to hurt the way we've been hurt. But Jesus asks us to do it differently. He took on all our wrongs so that we wouldn't have to bear the burdens of our transgressions. He asks that we do the same for others because "by his wounds we are healed." Shouldn't others receive that healing as well?

Praying you share forgiveness this week . . .

≣ Touchstones

Initial thoughts:

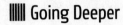 Going Deeper

Times I have wronged:

What I did in return:

Was it revenge or forgiveness?

How I feel when I truly forgive:

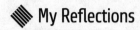 My Reflections

July

Lead me in your truth and teach me,

for you are the God of my salvation;

in you have I trusted all the day long.

Remember, O LORD, your compassion and love,

for they are from everlasting.

Psalm 25:4–5

In our liturgical calendar:

- The Season after Pentecost (Ordinary Time)

In our secular calendar:

- July 4—Independence Day
- Summer
- Vacations

JULY

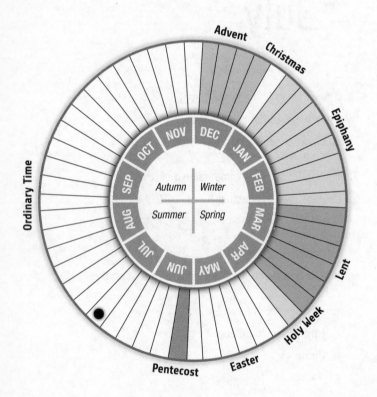

Week 28: Summer
(Ordinary Time)

Do you have any scars from when you were younger? I do—quite a few. There are scars from being completely careless and scars from events that were totally out of my control. Some of them were deeper and took longer to heal and some just seemed to go away. But each of those scars tells its own story and together they weave a bigger story. Life is like that. Events cause us to be hurt; sometimes so deeply that it takes longer to heal than other times.

Consider This:

We know that Christ has been raised from the dead and he will never die again. Death no longer has power over him.

Rom. 6:9

Even Jesus had scars; deep wounds that told the story of his life. Even after Jesus was raised from the dead, his scars remained with him. Life can be hard. We get hurt or we hurt others. But we are Easter people, believing fully in the Resurrection. Our life in Jesus will have wounds and those wounds will sometimes leave scars—scars that tell a story. But there is always the invitation of healing and with healing, new life.

Praying you find new life this week. . . .

≣ Touchstones

Initial thoughts:

||||| Going Deeper

The scars I can see are:

The scars I have that no one can see:

My visible scars tell this story:

My invisible scars tell this story:

My scars have made me stronger by . . .

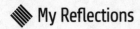 My Reflections

JULY

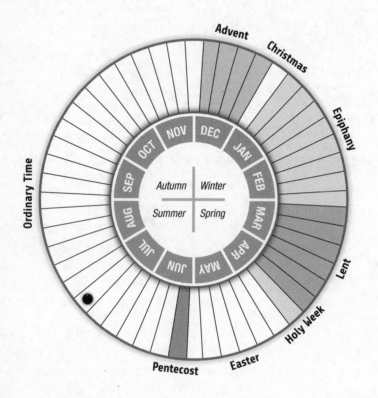

Week 29: Summer
(Ordinary Time)

Have you ever met those people where nothing is good? They always have a hurt or ailment, or there is a problem somewhere in their life almost all the time. Slowly over time, being around that kind of person can start to make you that way: cynical or snarky.

Consider This:

Get along well with God and be at peace; from this something good will come to you. Receive instruction from his mouth; put his words in your mind. If you return to the Almighty, you will be restored.

Job 22:21–23a

What if, when we encounter those people, we put God's words in our mind? I know we can't be a basket of joy every moment of every day, but we also don't have to listen to the complaints day after day. We can be encouraged by God's words and share them with others. There are messages of peace and joy throughout the Bible. What if we picked a few to remember and share the good feeling they give us? What if for just a moment, we could be a bright spot in someone's day?

Praying for you a bright spot this week . . .

☰ Touchstones

Initial thoughts:

||||| Going Deeper

I find myself complaining when:

How I react to other's complaints:

Ways I can use God's words to lift others or myself up:

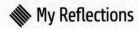 My Reflections

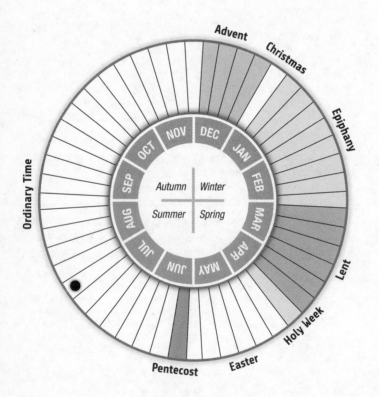

Week 30: Summer (Ordinary Time)

I t's the time of year for playtime on the water! On lakes, rivers, oceans, and pools with friends on boats, skis, boogie boards, surfboards, or floats. There are endless opportunities to splash around and enjoy the refreshing nature of water. But what about when the waters get rough?

Consider This:

One day Jesus and his disciples boarded a boat. He said to them, "Let's cross over to the other side of the lake." So they set sail. While they were sailing, he fell asleep. Gale-force winds swept down on the lake. The boat was filling up with water and they were in danger. So they went and woke Jesus, shouting, "Master, Master, we're going to drown!" But he got up and gave orders to the wind and the violent waves. The storm died down and it was calm. He said to his disciples, "Where is your faith?"

Luke 8:22–25a

Life is like that—calm one moment and stormy the next. We can be going along through our daily lives, doing our thing when out of the blue a storm rocks us. The storms look different for each person, but they are no less troubling. Jesus asks his disciples, "Where is your faith?" because he was with them and they panicked. I think we all do that to some extent until we are faced with the fact that Jesus is indeed always in our boat. We will not sink, we will not ever face those storms alone, and those storms will pass.

Praying for your calmness in the face of any storms this week . . .

≡ Touchstones

Initial thoughts:

▐▐▐ Going Deeper

The storms of my life are:

Times when I panic:

JULY

Time when I know Jesus is near:

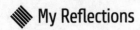 My Reflections

JULY

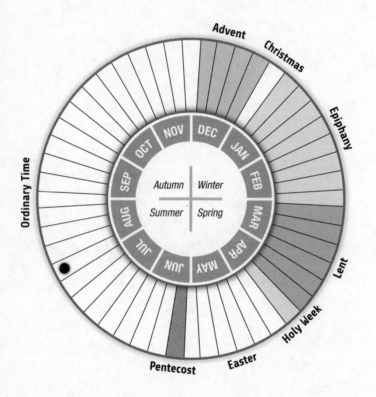

Week 31: Summer
(Ordinary Time)

What do you take with you when you travel? Do you pack too much, more than you ever use? Sometimes when I come home from traveling, most of the clothes I took weren't even worn. I try to pack light, but I feel like I need to cover all my bases and the "just in case" situations as well.

Consider This:

Jesus called the Twelve together and he gave them power and authority over all demons and to heal sicknesses. He sent them out to proclaim God's kingdom and to heal the sick. He told them, "Take nothing for the journey—no walking stick, no bag, no bread, no money, not even an extra shirt."

Luke 9:1–3

I think our society as a whole feels like we need more than we really do. Regardless of the fact that there is a store on every corner where we could purchase that thing we forgot, we need to take it with us and then don't use it. What would it be like to travel like Jesus asked the disciples to? Relying only on the kindness and hospitality of complete strangers? "Take nothing for the journey." Nothing! Not even money! Could you do it?

Praying for your having enough for the journey . . .

≣ Touchstones

Initial thoughts:

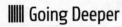 Going Deeper

Things I have to have when I travel:

How I feel when I forget them:

How it would feel to travel lighter:

How it would feel to live life lighter, with less stuff:

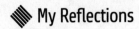 **My Reflections**

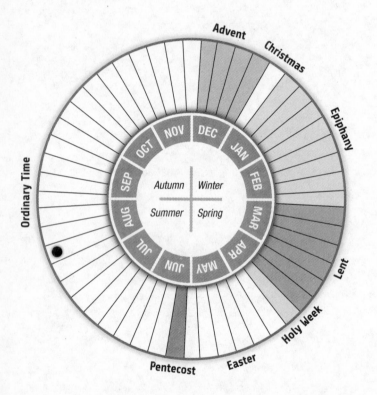

Week 32: Summer (Ordinary Time)

We're #1! We're the best! These are cheers you can hear at most sporting events, many times accompanied by a huge foam finger. Times like that are fun and I love them! But what does it really mean to be the best? Not everyone can be the "best," right? Isn't there only one "best" at any one thing?

Consider This:

Be the best in this work of grace in the same way that you are the best in everything, such as faith, speech, knowledge, total commitment, and the love we inspired in you.

2 Cor. 8:7

Our society pushes hard toward excellence in school, sports, clothing, electronics, and achievement. We don't think much about what we're actually doing in the moment and how that might help us grow in character and grace. Instead we're always focused on being the best and whatever we're doing to get us to the next thing. I'm not suggesting we don't try our best, but what if we tried to excel at grace first? What if our total commitment was to be graceful while doing our best and not what someone else has prescribed as our best? What if our main goal was to be as graceful toward others with as much effort as we put on other achievements?

Praying you enjoy the moments of today and the good work you have done this week . . .

≣ Touchstones

Initial thoughts:

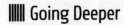 Going Deeper

What "grace" means to me:

Things at which I am the best:

Things at which I want to be the best:

How I can put grace before achievement and still be the best:

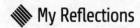 My Reflections

August

Everliving God, whose will it is that all should come to you through your Son Jesus Christ: Inspire our witness to him, that all may know the power of his forgiveness and the hope of his resurrection; who lives and reigns with you and the Holy Spirit, one God, now and for ever. Amen.

A Prayer for the Mission of the Church, BCP, 816

In our liturgical calendar:

- The Season after Pentecost (Ordinary Time)

In our secular calendar:

- Summer
- Back to school

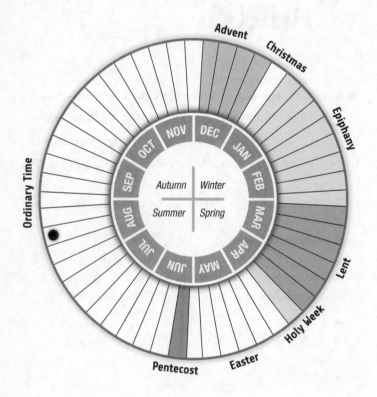

Week 33: Summer
(Ordinary Time)

Did your parent ever tell you to "share"? Do you know why? Why should we share at all? Can't I do with my stuff whatever I want to? What is mine is mine, right?

Consider This:

Tell people who are rich at this time not to become egotistical and not to place their hope on their finances, which are uncertain. Instead, they need to hope in God, who richly provides everything for our enjoyment. Tell them to do good, to be rich in the good things they do, to be generous, and to share with others.

1 Tim. 6:17–18

Do you know anyone who always seems to be giving stuff away or offering to help, to cook, or drive, or other generous offers? Those people seem to have figured out something that perhaps the rest of us could learn. Generosity isn't always about stuff so much as it is the heart with which it is given. There are so many things, gadgets, and "to-do" lists in life that we get distracted from the pure and simple joys around us. When we give from the heart, no matter the size of the offering, it matters greatly to God.

Praying you share generously this week . . .

≡ Touchstones

Initial thoughts:

||||| Going Deeper

Things I don't like to share:

How I feel when I openly share:

Times I don't acknowledge someone's need:

How I feel when I see a need and fill it:

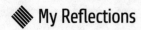 My Reflections

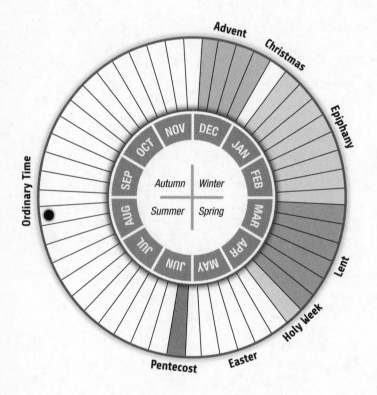

Week 34: Summer (Ordinary Time)

Have you started your back-to-school shopping yet? What's new? Or trending? What does "trending" even mean? The dictionary defines it as: "to emerge as a popular trend; be currently popular."[3] Even the news stations are getting in on it. *The Today Show* has a segment called "What's Trending." Really? I don't know about you, but I'm interested in something that's deeper, more genuine.

Consider This:

Do not be conformed to this world, but be transformed by the renewing of your minds, so that you may discern what is the will of God—what is good and acceptable and perfect.

Rom. 12:2 NRSV

Maybe that means that we shouldn't try so hard to conform to our culture that we fit into it without even thinking. Instead, we should fix our attention on God; be changed from the inside out. Then we can more easily recognize what God wants from us, and respond to it more naturally. Sometimes the culture around us can drag us down to its level of immaturity.

God brings out the best in us when we allow it—and then get out of the way.

Praying you have an exceptionally "unconforming" week . . .

---

3. Dictionary.com, s.v. "Trending," accessed December 28, 2015. http://dictionary.reference.com/browse/trending.

≡ Touchstones

Initial thoughts:

▌▌▌▌ Going Deeper

What is "trending" in my life:

Why that is important to me:

Where God is in the "trends" of my life:

How I can conform more to what God has in mind for me:

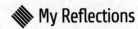 My Reflections

AUGUST

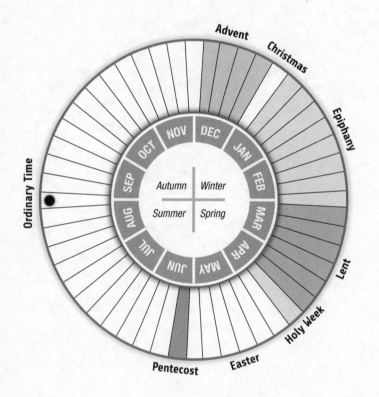

Week 35: Summer (*Ordinary Time*)

"No one has ever made himself great by showing how small someone else is."

—A quote attributed to Irvin Himmel[4]

Do you know anyone who does this? Maybe they do it without
even realizing it? It's hard when that happens. What do you do?
What can you do when you hear this happening to another?

Consider This:

*We who are strong ought to put up with the failings of the weak, and
not to please ourselves. Each of us must please our neighbor for the
good purpose of building up the neighbor.*

Rom. 15: 1–2 NRSV

What does that mean for us? I'm not sure, but maybe it means
I should lift up and support the things my friends are doing.
When they tell me something exciting, I should be excited with
them and jump on their "joy bandwagon." Lifting up others can
mean we hold back and don't talk about ourselves . . . at least
at that moment. Our time to shine can come later.

Praying you have a fantastic week with lots of chances to celebrate
your friends . . .

---

4. https://www.goodreads.com/quotes/953067-no-one-has-ever-made-
himself-great-by-showing-how

≡ Touchstones

Initial thoughts:

▓ Going Deeper

Times I am not really happy when others are successful:

Times I talk about myself when my friends tells me something wonderful about them:

Ways God can help me change that:

How I feel when I really celebrate someone else's success:

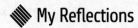 My Reflections

AUGUST

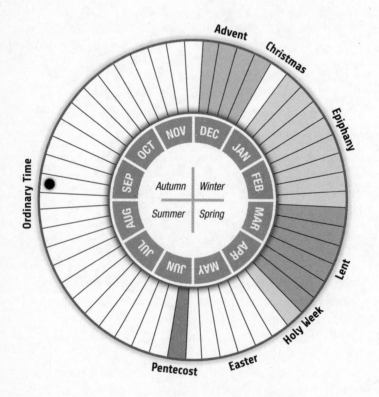

Week 36: Summer *(Ordinary Time)*

"Actions speak louder than words, but not nearly as often."
        —A quote attributed to Mark Twain[5]

We might hear that a lot, but what does it really mean? Have you ever had a friend tell you that they want to hang out but rarely can find the time or always offer an excuse? It is when someone says they will do something or shares they feel a certain way, but then they behave the opposite. That can be really hurtful when it happens to us. Especially from someone we care about.

Consider This:

Little children, let's not love with words or speech but with action and truth.

                  1 John 3:18

It's easy to talk about things, but it's harder to actually do them. But when we do follow through with what we say we will do, we build credibility, reliability, and trust. Remember the rainbow after the flood? That was God's promise not to flood the earth again. What if God had not followed through on that promise? Or had a change of mind or forgot? That sounds absurd, but that follow-through is what a covenant is; what a promise means. It is being true to yourself, true to your words, and all for the honor and glory of the God who keeps promises to us.

Praying you keep your promises this week . . .

---

5. http://www.goodreads.com/quotes/52502-action-speaks-louder-than-words-but-not-nearly-as-often

≡ Touchstones

Initial thoughts:

▥ Going Deeper

Times when my actions have been different than my words:

Times when a friend has done this to me:

How it feels:

How I can live in action and truth:

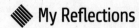 My Reflections

September

Give us grateful hearts, our Father, for all your mercies, and make us mindful of the needs of others; through Jesus Christ our Lord. Amen.

Grace at Meals, BCP, 835

In our liturgical calendar:

- The Season after Pentecost (Ordinary Time)

In our secular calendar:

- 1st Monday in September—Labor Day
- Back to school
- September 22 or 23—Autumnal (Fall) Equinox

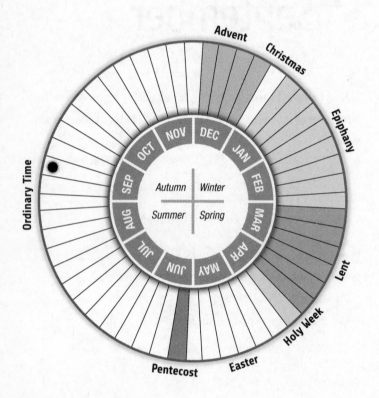

Week 37: School Starts
(Ordinary Time)

So, school has started and we're off and running! We might be at a new school or one we know. Maybe we're the new kid on the block, or have lots of old friends. Either way, we have a fresh start: a clean slate. What we do with it is up to us. We are in charge!

Consider This:

You will definitely enjoy what you've worked hard for—you'll be happy; and things will go well for you.

Ps. 128:2

Now, admittedly, we don't always get what we think we deserve when we work hard, but hard work makes us tired in a good way, knowing we have done our best. There is part of a prayer from the *New Zealand Prayer Book* that says: "What has been done has been done, let it be."[6] We can take comfort in that. So, do your best and know that God will be with you, no matter what.

Praying you enjoy the fruits of your hard work and that things go well for you . . .

---

6. "Night Prayer," *A New Zealand Prayer Book* (San Francisco: Harper Collins, 1997), 184.

≣ Touchstones

Initial thoughts:

||||| Going Deeper

Times when what other people thought was my best really wasn't:

Times I was celebrated for something that I didn't really deserve:

Times when I wasn't celebrated and should have been:

What is my best in God's eyes?

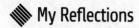 My Reflections

SEPTEMBER

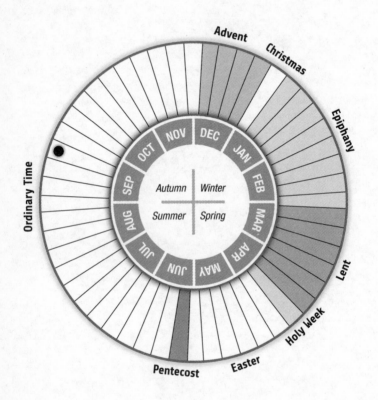

Week 38: Back to School
(*Ordinary Time*)

Lunch. The cafeteria can be weird, especially at a new school. Where do you go? Who do you sit with? What if your friends have a different lunch period? Then what? Our faith has a lot to say about food and meals and sharing.

Consider This:

I was hungry and you gave me food to eat. I was thirsty and you gave me a drink. I was a stranger and you welcomed me.

Matt. 25:35

Tables are natural gathering places. Inviting someone to join you can feel awkward, but it can also be a beautiful gift to someone. It shows acceptance and welcome. Even the school lunch table can be a holy place where we gather not only to eat, but to share and get to know each other better. It can also be a lonely place for those who might not have many friends. They may be the stranger Jesus is talking about. Who will you invite to eat with you?

Praying for opportunities for you to welcome the stranger to your table this week . . .

≡ Touchstones

Initial thoughts:

▋▋▋▋ Going Deeper

What is lunchtime like?

My routine challenges me because . . .

I see others eating alone and I . . .

How is God involved in inviting someone to have lunch?

My Reflections

SEPTEMBER

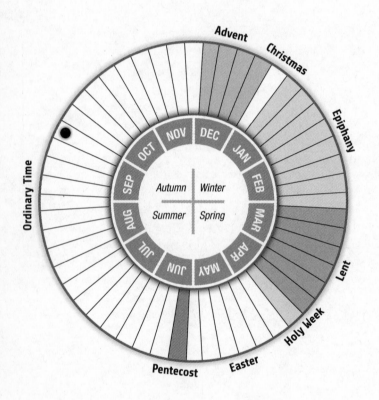

Week 39: Ordinary Time

Do you ever compare yourself to someone else? Wishing you had some aspect of the other person like body, hair, strength, or muscles?

Consider This:

No one ever hates his own body, but feeds it and takes care of it just like Christ does for the church.

Eph. 5:29

Maybe you work out, or try to eat healthy. I have friends who are vegetarians and swear I'll be healthier if I become one too. (I don't think that will happen—I like steak too much.) But I don't think that is what this passage is talking about. If we think of how Christ cares for the Church, it looks a whole lot different. I think it's a deeper caring. I think it's about what we feed our bodies, yes, but what we feed our minds and spirits too. I think it's about how we care for our whole selves, not just the physical part.

Praying you take extra good care of you this week . . .

≡ Touchstones

Initial thoughts:

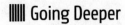 Going Deeper

Things I do that take care of my whole person:

Things I do that are not taking care of my whole person:

Parts of me that I neglect:

Small things I can do to take better care of me as one of God's creation:

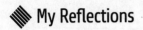

My Reflections

SEPTEMBER

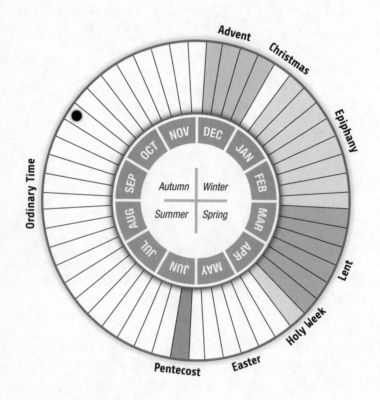

Week 40: Ordinary Time

Patience is hard. Technology malfunctions can make me want to pull my hair out. Patience with technology malfunctions . . . does that exist? Technology can be a really good thing. I'm a "techno-geek" and proudly so; however, when it doesn't work, I feel like throwing something out of the window. I experience even more frustration when online systems say things like: "Thanks for your patience while we fix . . ." Really? I don't have that patience! And, by the way, I'm not real happy about you inter-rupting my workflow! Does anything like this happen with you?

Consider This:

My brothers and sisters, think of the various tests you encounter as occasions for joy. After all, you know that the testing of your faith produces endurance. Let this endurance complete its work so that you may be fully mature, complete, and lacking in nothing.

James 1:2–4

Getting mad at a website or system seems silly, but we rely so heavily on these products in our lives that it's hard not to get frustrated. And this is just one life example. I think it's difficult to see those times as a gift or "occasion for joy" as it is sug-gested in James. But what if we could? What if we took that as an opportunity to just step away and get a new perspective? What if that challenge is a way of God reaching out to us to connect in a different way at that moment?

Praying you find a holy connection to God in those things that challenge you this week . . .

≣ Touchstones

Initial thoughts:

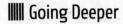 Going Deeper

Things that really try my patience:

People who test my patience:

SEPTEMBER

Why do they?

Times I am easily able to be patient:

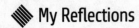

My Reflections

October

Grant us, Lord, not to be anxious about earthly things, but to love things heavenly; and even now, while we are placed among things that are passing away, to hold fast to those that shall endure; through Jesus Christ our Lord, who lives and reigns with you and the Holy Spirit, one God, for ever and ever. Amen.

Collect for Proper 20, BCP, 234

In our liturgical calendar:

- The Season after Pentecost (Ordinary Time)
- October 4—The Feast of St. Francis

In our secular calendar:

- 2nd Monday in October—Columbus Day
- October 31—All Hallows' Eve (Halloween)

OCTOBER

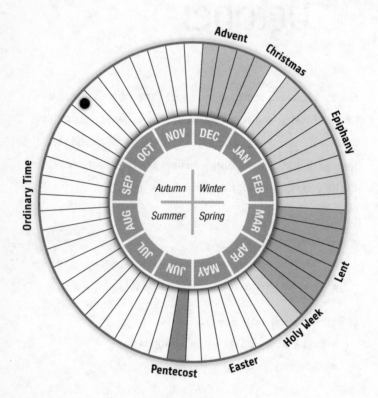

Week 41: The Feast of St. Francis of Assisi (Ordinary Time)

October 4th is the Feast of St. Francis. On the Sunday closest to that, we celebrate the Feast by hosting a Blessing of the Animals. We follow this practice because Francis is considered the patron saint of animals, perhaps because of the story attributed to St. Francis and the Wolf of Gubbio.[7] In the story, Francis goes in search of a vicious wolf that has terrorized the town in order to make peace with it. The wolf has been haunting the town due to extreme hunger. With Francis as the mediator, the wolf and the town make a pact—a promise of peace. The town promises to feed the wolf and the wolf promises never to hurt anyone. Seems like it was originally a big misunderstanding from the very beginning.

Have you ever been misunderstood like the wolf? Have you ever needed a mediator like Francis was for the wolf? Have you needed someone to help facilitate a conversation for you because you have been misunderstood?

I think misunderstandings happen more than we think. Especially since a lot of conversations happen electronically. We can't see the eyes of the other person or hear their voice. We see and hear only what our hearts and hurt feelings allow. Next time you begin to feel misunderstood, meet them face-to-face before you respond. It will help in the long run.

Praying that you have very few misunderstandings . . .

---

7. Sharon Callahan, "St. Francis and the Wolf of Gubbio," accessed October 6, 2015, www.anaflora.com/articles/saints-sages/saint-1.html.

≣ Touchstones

Initial thoughts:

IIIII Going Deeper

Times I have been misunderstood:

Times I have helped mediate for others:

Times I knew God was present even though I was misunderstood:

▨ My Reflections

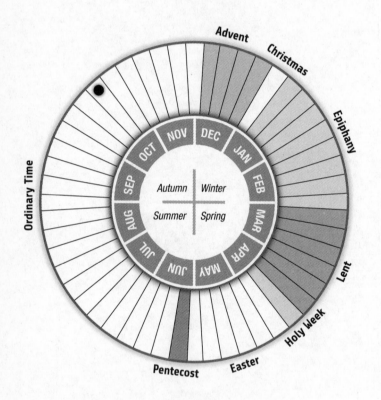

Week 42: Ordinary Time

Do you ever complain? (I do! Sometimes a lot!) When do you complain the most? Why do we complain? Is it because things aren't going as we planned or envisioned?

Sometimes things don't go as we planned and it can be frustrating. Plans change. Events may not unfold as we had hoped. Life will throw us some curveballs. People will let us down.

Consider This:

Do everything without grumbling and arguing.

Phil. 2:14

Seriously? It's hard, isn't it? But God never promises us that life will be easy, only that God will be present with us at all times and that our complaints will be heard.

Praying for you an easy and complaint-free week . . .

≣ Touchstones

Initial thoughts:

 Going Deeper

When I complain the most:

Why I complain:

How I feel when others complain:

How I feel when I take my complaints to God:

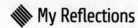 My Reflections

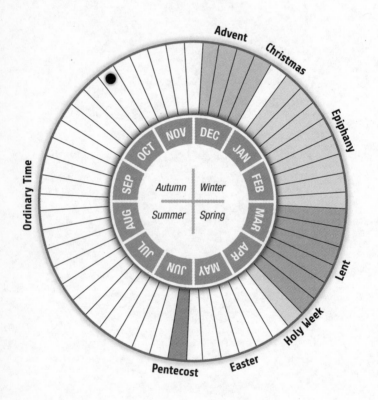

Week 43: Ordinary Time

"**idk**" Really? Do you ever text that to friends or family? I do. And sometimes it is because I'm not sure they want to hear the real answer. Could it be that maybe we're afraid to take a stand on what we think? Has that ever happened to you?

Consider This:

Where did John get his authority to baptize? Did he get it from heaven or from humans? They argued among themselves, "If we say 'from heaven,' he'll say to us, 'Then why didn't you believe him?' But we can't say 'from humans' because we're afraid of the crowd, since everyone thinks John was a prophet." Then they replied, "We don't know."

Matt. 21:25–27

Clearly this happened even in the Bible. Sometimes I think the apostles (Jesus's friends) gave Jesus a headache more than once. But it just shows me that even with Jesus to hang out with in person, answering, "I don't know" was easier than taking a chance on saying what they really thought.

Praying for you a humble heart and honest answers . . .

≡ Touchstones

Initial thoughts:

▥ Going Deeper

What are the uncomfortable conversations I avoid?

How can I allow God to give me the courage to speak the real truth?

How I react when I hear a truth I don't want to hear:

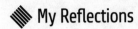 My Reflections

OCTOBER

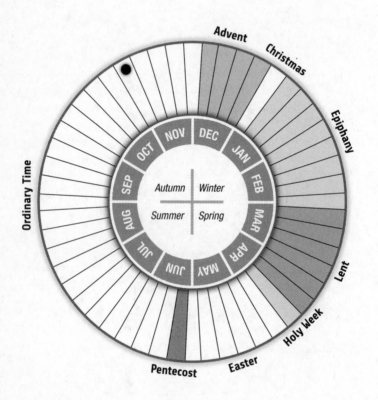

Week 44: Ordinary Time

Have you ever met anyone that has to be right all the time, correcting everything you say? Have you ever been that way? When we act as though we know everything about a particular subject (even though we actually might), we can get prideful. It somehow makes us feel bad to be wrong, so we try really hard to be right. And, if someone is arguing a point with us and we know the right answer, we need them to acknowledge to us that we are right. It can become a vicious circle that can harm relationships.

Consider This:

Avoid godless and pointless discussions and the contradictory claims of so-called "knowledge." When some people adopted this false knowledge, they missed the goal of faith.

1 Tim. 6:20b–21

Sometimes I think we get so caught up in being right that we forget what is more important. Is it okay to let your friend go on about a topic, sharing information that is inaccurate? Do you need to make them see the error of their ways? What if the subject is about God or your faith? It is always a good thing to share your love of God with another and to invite someone to get to know Christ, to visit your church or faith home. But there are people who might challenge what you believe. Let them. When you know who you are and whose you are, being right doesn't matter. What matters is showing them the face of Christ in that moment through you, your actions, and your words.

Praying for you easy conversations this week . . .

≡ Touchstones

Initial thoughts:

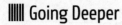 ## Going Deeper

I hate being wrong when:

I want others to know I'm right because:

How I turn to God in these times:

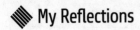 My Reflections

OCTOBER

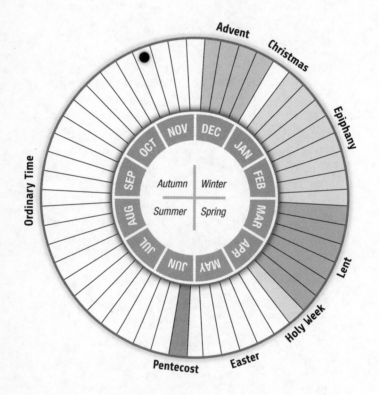

Week 45: All Hallows' and All Saints' Days

Halloween is a time of contradictions. It is a both/and time that has deep ancient roots.

October 31st is Halloween or All Hallows' Eve, when children (and some adults) dress up in costume and celebrate with parties or roaming the neighborhood "trick-or-treating." Some say the tradition comes from a time the souls of the dead were thought to revisit their homes. Feasts were had, at which the souls of dead relatives were beckoned to attend, with a place set at the table for them. Mumming (performing) and guising (wearing a disguise) were part of the festival, and involved people going door-to-door, often reciting verses of Scripture in exchange for food (treats).

The following day, November 1, is All Saints' Day, when we remember the saints, known and unknown, and the faithful departed believers.

Consider This:

I assure you that they gave what they could afford and even more than they could afford, and they did it voluntarily. They urgently begged us for the privilege of sharing in this service for the saints.

2 Cor. 8:3-4

Halloween is fun, sometimes really fun! With the rising sun brings All Saints' Day and a time of remembrance. As you think of your loved ones who are no longer at the table, also remember the saints that have had the privilege of serving in your life and have offered all that we see in our midst.

Praying you get the treats of love and wonder as we remember our saints this week . . .

▤ Touchstones

Initial thoughts:

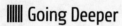 Going Deeper

My favorite Halloween treats:

My favorite Halloween activities:

The saints in my life:

Why I consider them saints:

The saints I no longer see:

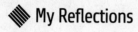 My Reflections

November

O gracious Father, who opens your hand and fills all things living with plenteousness: Bless the lands and waters, and multiply the harvests of the world; let your Spirit go forth, that it may renew the face of the earth; show your loving-kindness, that our land may give her increase; and save us from selfish use of what you give, that men and women everywhere may give you thanks; through Christ our Lord. Amen.

Prayer for the Harvest of Lands and Waters, BCP, 828

In our liturgical calendar:

- The Season after Pentecost (Ordinary Time)
- November 1—All Saints' Day
- November 2—All Souls' Day
- Advent begins

In our secular calendar:

- 1st Tuesday in November—Election Day
- November 11—Veteran Day
- 4th Thursday in November—Thanksgiving Day

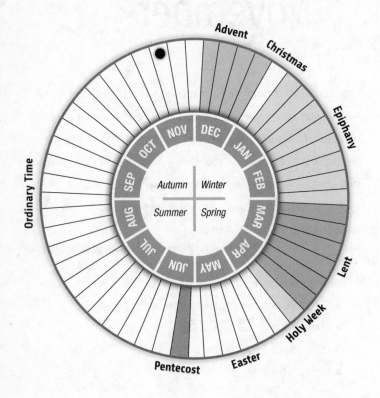

Week 46: Ordinary Time

Have you ever been in a rut? When you just do the same thing, eat the same thing, hang with the same people, or go to the same places—all the time? Predictability like that can be comforting or boring, or cause us to miss the sacred moments right in front of us.

Do you ever get so involved in your day-to-day tasks that you don't even notice the "new" around you? Or maybe there is an event or activity you won't try (or repeat) because you have a preconceived notion about it. I'm guilty, and I've missed some really cool "holy happenings" because of it.

When we were very young, everything was new and delightful. We discovered that every turn held a new and unexpected surprise. Discovery is not only about exploring to find something new about an event, place, person, or activity—it's about discovering something new within you. It is also about being open to the sacred in everyday life.

Consider This:

People were bringing babies to Jesus so that he would bless each of them. When the disciples saw this, they scolded them. Then Jesus called them to him and said, "Allow the children to come to me. Don't forbid them, because God's kingdom belongs to people like these children."

Luke 18:15–16

God wants us to come like little children, full of delight at our discovery of the Creation. God has a way of surprising us in the most delightful ways and may even have a good surprise in store for you today.

Praying for you holy discoveries and many delights this week . . .

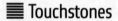 Touchstones

Initial thoughts:

IIIII Going Deeper

Routine things that keep me "stuck":

How I can break out of that:

Things I am willing to give a second chance:

 My Reflections

NOVEMBER

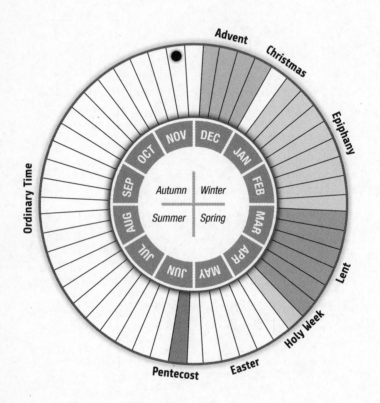

Week 47: Ordinary Time

Our church recently began to set aside space where people can come and be quiet. They are invited to bring a book of their own or nothing, to follow along in the prayer guide provided, or do their own prayer. Either way, it is "a sacred space" set aside in the busyness of life to just be quiet.

Consider This:

Be still, and know that I am God!

Ps. 46:10a NIV

and this:

Come to me, all you that are struggling hard and carrying heavy loads, and I will give you rest.

Matt. 11:28

When do you set aside time to just "be"? To be quiet and away from all noise and distractions? To refresh yourself and your spirit?

I invite you to find a quiet spot this week to feel God's presence with you.

Praying for you a "sacred space" this week . . .

▤ Touchstones

Initial thoughts:

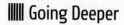 Going Deeper

Reasons I don't set time aside for myself:

Reasons I don't set time aside for God:

Things that keep me distracted from "just being":

How I can schedule my time differently:

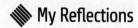 My Reflections

NOVEMBER

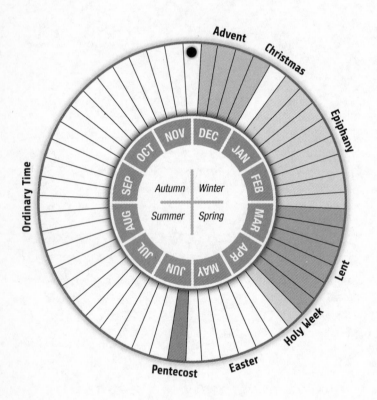

Week 48: Thanksgiving
(Ordinary Time)

Thanksgiving will be here soon. It is one of those holidays where food seems to be the star of the show.

Consider This:

The disciples asked each other, "Has someone brought him food?" Jesus said to them, "I am fed by doing the will of the one who sent me and by completing his work. Don't you have a saying, 'Four more months and then it's time for harvest'? Look, I tell you: open your eyes and notice that the fields are already ripe for the harvest.

John 4:33–35

Of course our bodies need food for energy and nourishment, but there is so much more to being fed. Being in the kitchen cooking, talking, and laughing is one of my most fond memories of big holidays. It feeds me in a special way, but I don't think that is what Jesus is talking about. It does nourish our spirits to be together and share a meal, but I don't think that is what Jesus was talking about. I believe Jesus means that when we do what we are deeply called to do, what God has put in front of us to do, we are fed in such a way that our spiritual cup truly overflows with a joy only that work can bring. And for each of us, that work is different, but collaborative. Open your eyes. Look around. What work do you need to do? What work do we need to do? My work is different from your work and vice versa, but I can't do my work without you by my side doing your work.

Praying you find joy in the work you have to do this week . . .

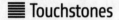 Touchstones

Initial thoughts:

▥ Going Deeper

The work I feel deeply called to do:

Things I do that drain my spirit:

NOVEMBER

Things I do that feed my spirit:

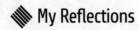 My Reflections

NOVEMBER

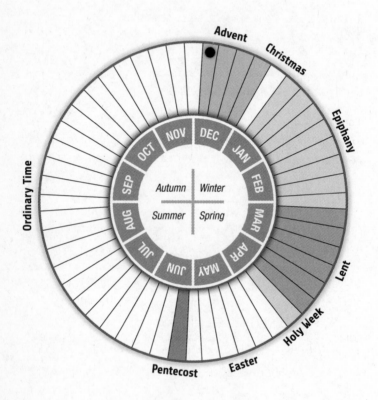

Week 49: Advent 1

Waiting . . . it's one of my least favorite things to do—but sometimes it is inevitable. I love it when I get all the green lights on the way home, or when there is no one in line at the grocery store, or if I text someone a question and get an immediate reply.

Consider This:

Happy are those servants whom the master finds waiting up when he arrives.

Luke 12:37

The Bible talks a lot about waiting. It seems to run through a lot of the stories, especially as we enter the season of Advent. Waiting asks that we be patient and that is really hard sometimes. You might be late to class or to work, and if that person in front of you would just move, you could get on with what you need to do!

But it can have its advantages. What if we chose to wait differently? What if we chose to discover that person in line ahead of us? What if we just took a moment to take in our surroundings, to be aware and give thanks? What would we find out about ourselves?

It's Advent. It's time to wait on the delivery of God's only Son to us. As we enter this holy season, take time to discover the person next to you. Take a moment to look around and give thanks.

Praying you find new discoveries in the waiting . . .

≡ Touchstones

Initial thoughts:

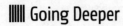 Going Deeper

The hardest part of waiting for me is:

How I express my dissatisfaction in having to wait:

How I can choose to look for God when I have to wait:

How I feel about waiting for God to come into the world as a baby:

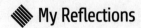 My Reflections

December

Eternal Father, you gave to your incarnate Son the holy name of Jesus to be the sign of our salvation: Plant in every heart, we pray, the love of him who is the Savior of the world, our Lord Jesus Christ; who lives and reigns with you and the Holy Spirit, one God, in glory everlasting. Amen.

Collect for the Holy Name (January 1), BCP, 213

In our liturgical calendar:

- The Season of Advent
- The Season of Christmas

In our secular calendar:

- December 21 or 22—Winter Solstice
- December 25—Christmas
- December 31—New Year's Eve

DECEMBER

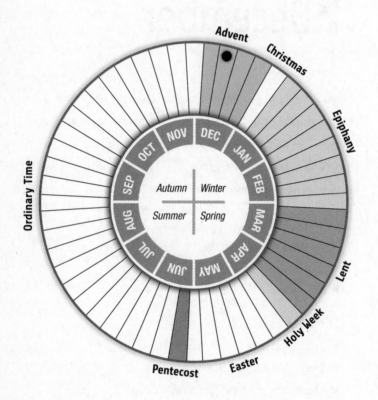

Week 50: Advent 2

Have you ever been with a group of your friends that just won't listen? Maybe there's something you feel strongly about or something you really need to share and they just won't listen. Or maybe it's because we don't feel like we can say it well enough. Sometimes we know what we need to say, but just can't get the words right. It can be really frustrating.

Consider This:

"Go and tell Pharaoh, Egypt's king, to let the Israelites out of his land." But Moses said to the LORD, "The Israelites haven't even listened to me. How can I expect Pharaoh to listen to me, especially since I'm not a very good speaker?"

Exod. 6:11–12

Moses had a really big job. God wanted him to go to the man in charge and make demands. Can you imagine? His friends wouldn't even listen to him; why in the world would the guy in charge listen to him, especially since he didn't think he could get the words right?

Listening is a gift we can give to others even if we don't understand them. It is also a great gift to receive. Communication, in general, is one of those tricky things because you never really know what the other person is thinking or feeling. It's one of those places in life where you just have to do your best. So next time you notice someone trying to say something in a group that doesn't seem to hear them . . . listen. Give them your attention. It is probably one of the most simple and kind gifts you can offer.

Praying you are listening this week . . .

 ## Touchstones

Initial thoughts:

▌▌▌ Going Deeper

Times when I find myself interrupting to say what I want to say:

Times I'm afraid to speak my mind in front of my friends:

How I can help my friends feel heard:

I listen best to God when:

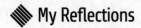 My Reflections

DECEMBER

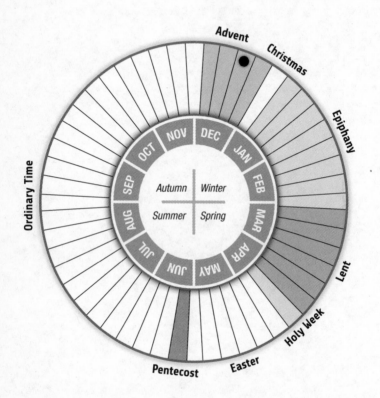

Week 51: Advent 3

This time of year is a little crazy for everyone. There are presents to buy, parties to attend, family to visit, and cookies to be baked. The list goes on and on. We get so stressed out by long lines and heavy traffic that we forget that everyone else is out there doing exactly what we are doing—getting ready for Christmas!

Consider This:

Nothing is impossible for God.

Luke 1:37

But what should we really be doing to get ready for Christmas? What was this time like for Mary, Jesus's mother? Can you imagine? Getting ready for a baby that was God's son—fully divine and fully human. It sounds impossible! But Mary believed and agreed to be a part of this holy experience, no matter the personal cost. What if we did that just a little? What if we allowed ourselves to believe that nothing is impossible for God? Really believe?

Praying you see the impossible become possible . . .

≣ Touchstones

Initial thoughts:

IIIII Going Deeper

Things I think are impossible for me:

Things I would do if I knew I couldn't fail:

Things I think are possible if I let God handle them:

Things I will do to ready my heart for the coming of the Holy Christ Child:

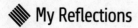 My Reflections

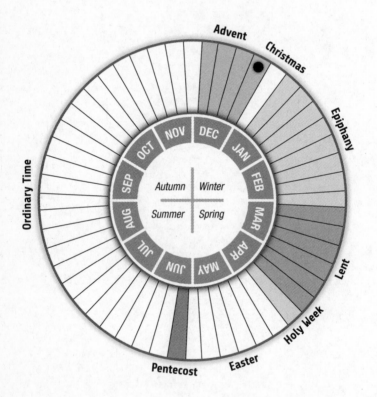

Week 52: Advent 4
(Christmas)

I love Christmas! I love it for all the reasons you can think of, but those reasons have changed over the years as times have changed. Our traditions have changed as new family members join us through marriage, birth, or friendship and as family members have passed away, but there are a few traditions that stand firm.

Consider This:

God called all of you through our good news so you could possess the honor of our Lord Jesus Christ. So then, brothers and sisters, stand firm and hold on to the traditions we taught you, whether we taught you in person or through our letter. Our Lord Jesus Christ himself and God our Father loved us and through grace gave us eternal comfort and a good hope. May he encourage your hearts and give you strength in every good thing you do or say.

2 Thess. 2:14–17

I'm sure most of us get caught up in the trappings of Christmas with all the decorations, Santa visits, presents, shopping, cooking, and seasonal TV specials. Those things are fun, but they are distracting from what is really the "reason for the season." Traditions are important. We should all have them, especially during Christmas. But what if we looked at all those things and activities differently? What if we set an intention around all we did during the preparation of and eventual arrival of Christ-mas? What if we deeply embraced our families with joy while we shopped, cooked, and watched those TV specials? What if we acknowledged that the love we share with others through those activities is the love God showed for us in preparing a way for God's Son to enter our world? What if we shifted from feeling stressed about getting it all done, to really allowing joy to guide us through the waiting for and preparing for and receiving the Christ child?

Praying for you firm traditions filled with joy . . .

≣ Touchstones

Initial thoughts:

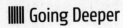 Going Deeper

My family traditions:

Ones I wish would go away:

Ones I want to do forever:

Why I love my favorite ones:

Times I feel God near during Christmas:

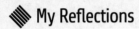 My Reflections